RUNNING'S
STRANGEST®
TALES

RUNNING'S
STRANGEST®
TALES

Extraordinary but true tales from over
five centuries of running

IAIN SPRAGG

PORTICO

First published in the United Kingdom in 2016 by
Portico
1 Gower Street
London
WC1E 6HD

An imprint of Pavilion Books Company Ltd

ISBN 978-1-91023-292-7

A CIP catalogue record for this book is available from the British Library.

10 9 8 7 6 5 4 3 2 1

Reproduction by Colourdepth UK
Printed and bound by Bookwell, Finland

Illustrations by Matthew Booker

This book can be ordered direct from the publisher at www.pavilionbooks.com

CONTENTS

We run, not because we think it is doing us good, but because we enjoy it and cannot help ourselves. The more restricted our society and work become, the more necessary it will be to find some outlet for this craving for freedom. No one can say, 'You must not run faster than this, or jump higher than that.' The human spirit is indomitable.

(Sir Roger Bannister)

INTRODUCTION

Ever since mankind stood tall and proud on his and her two feet, people have been running here, there and everywhere and when it comes to getting from A to B in the quickest time possible, running has got its old rival walking beaten all ends up.

In its earliest incarnations running was no more than a practical necessity for those not blessed with horses or other more rapid forms of transport, but over the years it has grown into the most popular physical pastime on the planet, a global phenomenon that sees millions from London to the Lebanon and Manchester to Macau lace up their trainers every day and get a sweat on.

The Ancient Greeks really put running on the map with the advent of the first Olympic Games nearly 3,000 years ago, and ever since they popularised the sport, men and women have been gallivanting about hither and thither as fast as their two legs will carry them

Running's Strangest Tales celebrates the enduring popularity of the sport, but more importantly it remembers its most unconventional characters from over the centuries, the most bizarre races and the inevitable but hilarious mishaps and misfortunes that have afflicted elite and amateur athletes alike.

And so, in the pages which follow, you can read all about Britain's seventeenth-century 'freak races' featuring cripples, men on stilts and fishmongers carrying *fruits de mer* on their heads and the remarkable and plucky Alfred 'Alfie' Shrubb, a man who once broke seven world records in a single race.

There is the tale of the ultramarathoner Marshall Ulrich and his eye-watering decision to have his toenails surgically removed in pursuit of faster times and the story of the British madman who ran the thousand and more miles between John O'Groats and Land's End with a fridge strapped to his back.

Other running curios include the Japanese athlete who took more than 54 years to complete an Olympic marathon, the hapless Norwegian footballer who had a rather unfortunate encounter with a moose while out for a jog and the 'Impossible 5K' race in America, an event in which competitors improbably complete the course *before* they've actually started.

To complete the feast of athletic mayhem, there is also the intoxicating tale of the Italian runner who refused to race before finishing off a bottle of Chianti and the story of the redoubtable Lily Groom, the 1920s housewife who ran from London to Brighton pushing her pram all the way.

Running's Strangest Tales is essential reading for anyone who has even only once decided to pick up the pace and see how fast they could go and hilarious proof that running can frequently be a dangerous, controversial and bizarre pastime.

Iain Spragg

THE SWINGING GREEKS

GREECE, 720BC

Ever since *Homo erectus* decided to think outside the box nearly two million years ago, abandoning the traditional all-fours approach to perambulation and standing proud on two legs, men and women throughout the millennia have been running.

Back in the prehistoric day, running was no more than a perfunctory business, a way to escape the clutches of an irate sabre-toothed tiger perhaps, or to hasten back to the family cave after realising you'd accidentally left the fire on.

The concept of running for pleasure rather than necessity came much later in mankind's story and it is with some authority the Ancient Greeks can claim to have transformed athletic pumping of the legs into both a competitive event and a leisure activity with the advent of the Olympic Games. Suddenly running was no longer merely a means of rapidly getting from A to B, it was a spectator sport.

The first Olympics were held in 776BC but it was at the Games 56 years later that the history of running took its first bizarre turn when a Greek athlete by the name of Orsippus from Megara entered the *stadion*, a race estimated to be held over a distance of 190m (207¾ yards) and, like its modern 100m descendant, very much the blue ribbon event of proceedings.

Orsippus was nothing if not an innovator, and in a first

for the Games, decided to ditch his clothes and run in the *stadion* starkers. In the buff. Completely naked.

It was a bold move. There are of course obvious aerodynamic advantages to be had from disrobing but it's a moot point whether they would be negated by the increased, ahem, 'downstairs bounce' that inevitably resulted. There was though evidently method in Orsippus' madness and he romped home in first place.

'My own opinion is that at Olympia he intentionally let the girdle slip off him,' argued the writer Pausanias in his book *Description of Greece*, 'realizing that a naked man can run more easily than one girt.'

As with much ancient history however there is controversy when it comes to Orsippus' claim to be the first naked Olympic champion and others have named a chap called Acanthus of Sparta as the Games' original competitive streaker.

Acanthus competed at the same Olympics as Orsippus in the *diaulos* (approximately 400m) and *dolichos* (roughly 4,800m) events and if we are to believe the Greek historian Dionysius of Halicarnassus and his tome *Roman Antiquities*, he's our man.

'After the chariots came the competitors ...*gymnoi* [naked] for the rest of their bodies but with their genitals covered,' he wrote. 'This custom was still observed in my time in Rome ... It is now ended in Greece, and the Spartans ended it. The person who first removed his clothing and ran *gymnos* was Acanthus ... Before that time all the Greeks considered it shameful to appear in the games with their bodies entirely *gymna*.'

We'll probably never know definitively which of the two got their kit off first but we can say the 720BC Games were the least inhibited in Olympic history.

Incidentally, the Greek word *stadion* has given us the modern word 'stadium', so while most of us have not inherited their penchant for nude running, we are indebted to them for that particular etymological legacy.

WAR GAMES

GREECE, 520BC

The Greeks were a fickle bunch when it came to their athletics. We have just explored the origins of naked running at the Olympics in the previous entry and now we shall delve into how, just 200 years later, they underwent a weighty *volte-face* and decided to have competitors at the Games gallivanting around and about the stadium in full body armour.

The year is 520BC, it's the sixty-fifth instalment of the Olympics, and for the first time the Games witnesses an event called the *hoplitodromos* (rough English translation, 'race of soldiers'), in which entrants dashed along a course measuring between 350 and 400m (383–437 yards), kitted out in the helmet, bronze-covered wooden shield and metal shin guards which Greek infantrymen commonly wore in battle. Racers were spared having to strap on the *cuirass* – the soldier's metal breastplate – but nonetheless the whole kit was estimated to weigh in at around 50lb (22.7kg). It's like asking Usain Bolt to sprint clutching a microwave.

In the interests of historical accuracy it is important to point out competitors were still starkers aside from all the armour but it does all rather beg the question what was the point of clanking around the course, if you'll excuse the mixed military analogy, in full metal jacket?

The answer can be found 30 years earlier when a Persian army invaded Greece. The impertinent Persians had massed ranks of rather deadly archers but the Greek infantry equipped themselves with distinction against the aerial bombardment, charging the lines at full speed to take the enemy by surprise.

The introduction of the *hoplitodromos* to the Olympics was both a celebration of their exploits and an on-going exercise for possible future skirmishes.

'The run in armour was introduced as an athletic competition and, at the same time, to train *hoplites* for running in armour,' wrote historian Nick Sekunda in *Marathon 490BC: The First Persian Invasion of Greece*. 'It seems the *hoplite* [soldier] would not be expected to run further than this distance [360m] and that they began their charge at the run two stades away from the Persian line. This is precisely when … they would have come within effective range of the Persian Army.'

Or as third-century Greek writer Philostratus pithily put it, athletes 'regarded war as training for gymnastics, and gymnastics as training for war'.

The problem was the *hoplitodromos* was not always the edifying sight the Games organisers hoped for as the runners dropped their shields in the hustle and bustle of a race and often tumbled over. Things were further complicated by the fact there was a hairpin turn on the Olympic course and competitors had to grab hold of a wooden post – the *kampter* – to help them negotiate the tight bend while still clutching their shields. If they all arrived at the *kampter* at the same time, it was bedlam.

The modern equivalent of the *hoplitodromos* would be the policeman's 100m dash in full riot gear, an impromptu event staged whenever rumours of free Krispy Kremes spread through the ranks.

THE MADNESS OF THE MARATHON MONKS

JAPAN, 788AD

The pursuit of spiritual and religious enlightenment and the search for the meaning of life is a frustratingly elusive business. While countless charlatans have claimed to have unlocked the secret (which they're more than happy to share subject to full disclosure of your mother's maiden name and your credit card details), the general consensus is that a Zen-like higher state of consciousness is jolly hard to achieve.

Many runners of course experience a certain sense of clarity and calmness, albeit not exactly a religious epiphany, while clocking up the miles, but they really can't hold a torch to the famed Marathon Monks of Mount Hiei, who go to extraordinary lengths – not to mention distances – in their quest to attain enlightenment.

Ours monks are Tendai Buddhists in Japan, and ever since their Enryaku-ji monastery was founded on Mount Hiei, in the mountains north of Kyoto back in 788, they've been embarking on a gruelling athletic rite of passage, which begs as many questions about their sanity as it reveals the depths of their religious devotion.

It takes seven years to complete their Herculean task, known as the *kaihogyo*, and requires the monks to complete the equivalent of 1,000 marathons in 1,000 days. They walk or run at night, stopping at a series of temples and shrines along the way to pray and recite ritual chants, and there's not a water station or St John Ambulance in sight.

To further up the ante, the monks must complete their task wearing straw sandals, rather than a nice comfy pair of Nike Airs and, at the end of the whole thing, they're required to retire to a darkened room for nine days without food, water or sleep and contemplate what they have learned. And their multiple blisters.

It is, we can all agree, a beast of a challenge and between 1885 and 2015 a mere 46 monks successfully completed the gruelling *kaihogyo*.

'It is a time to meditate on life, on how you should live,' explained one of the monks in John Stevens' book *The Marathon Monks of Mount Hiei*. 'All humans are asking the question, "Why are we alive?" The constant movement for 1,000 days gives you lots of time to think about this, to reflect on your life. It is a type of meditation through movement.'

Those rare, exhausted few who do finish the *kaihogyo* become national celebrities, with the final stages of their exploits broadcast live to the country, an unsurprising addition to the infamously sadistic TV schedules in Japan, which have variously featured game show contestants being slapped in the testicles, forced to live in solitary confinement for a year or having blow darts fired at their bared buttocks. Crazy country, Japan.

THE FORGOTTEN FOOTMEN

UK, 1450s

Professional long distance runners can make a handsome living these days from their natural ability to get from A to B in the quickest time possible, but one of the first groups to earn a crust for jogging for prolonged periods were known as the running footmen, and those poor sods had it tough.

The first running footmen appeared in the mid-fifteenth century. Their job was to accompany the horse-drawn carriages transporting wealthy toffs on their journeys, clearing obstacles from the road, helping free the carriages should they become stuck, and running ahead to alert the local innkeeper that Mr and Mrs St John-Smythe would be with them shortly and would be requiring roast grouse and a nice claret for dinner.

Running footmen quickly became a status symbol – the more you employed, the posher you were, and the really big cheeses could have up to six trotting ahead of their carriages as they travelled up and down the country.

The problem was, as the years went by, the job became harder and harder. Fifteenth-century carriages rolled at a relatively modest 5mph (8km/h) due to the terrible state of the roads (council budgets for road repairs were minuscule even back then), but as the quality of the highways and byways steadily improved, the coaches got faster and faster and the later generations of unfortunate running footmen had to keep up.

By the late eighteenth century the carriages were estimated to be doing a heady 7mph (11.3km/h) and our human outriders were expected to run up to 60 miles (96.6km/h) a day, often clocking up 20 miles (32.2km) without a break. All while simultaneously bowing and scraping to the pampered passengers inside the carriage.

Unsurprisingly many running footmen simply keeled over and died from sheer exhaustion. Others shuffled off this mortal coil after three or four years' service after contracting tuberculosis, a condition possibly brought on by consistently breathing in the dusty air created by the passage of the carriages. Those mortalities gave rise to the erroneous eighteenth-century belief that running was bad for the health.

An onerous life indeed, but to add insult to injury, their monied employers often raced the running footmen against each other for sport and entertainment. The toffs of course couldn't resist betting on proceedings.

'In the evening rode out to Woodstock Park, where saw a race between Groves (Duke of Wharton's running footman) and Phillips (Diston's),' wrote one Sir Erasmus Phillips in his diary in 1720. 'My namesake ran the 4 miles [6.4km] round the course in 18 min and won the race, thereby his master £1,000, the sum he and Groves started for. On this occasion there was a most prodigious concourse of people.'

As far as we know Groves and Phillips emerged from this race unscathed but it was not always the case.

'In the eighteenth century footmen were frequently matched to race against horses and carriages,' wrote William Shepard Walsh in *A Handy Book of Curious Information*. 'One of the last recorded contests was in 1770, between a famous running man and the Duke of Marlborough, the latter wagering that in his phaeton [carriage] and four [horse] he would beat the footman in a race from London to Windsor. The poor footman worn out by his exertions and much chagrined by his defeat died, it was said, of over fatigue.'

Just to clarify, that's 25-odd miles (40.2km) for our sadly departed footman against a top-of-the-range coach pulled by four thoroughbred horses. The poor bugger never stood a chance.

BRAWLING BO PEEPS

GERMANY, 1650s

The Germans are an innately competitive race and when it comes to car manufacturing, penalty shootouts or the precision placement of beach towels in order to claim the coveted sun loungers closest to the pool, our Teutonic cousins undeniably like to win. They may come up short in the sense of humour stakes but no one's perfect.

This burning desire to be victorious is perfectly illustrated by the historical 'Shepherdess Race' held in the rural town of Markgröningen in the south-west of Germany. It's an event which survives to this day, but back in the seventeenth century it was a rather rowdy and physical affair.

The origins of the race actually date back to the mid-fifteenth century, when the shepherds of Markgröningen began the annual tradition of legging it across a 263 yard (240m) course set out on a stubble field. To prove their manliness, they did this barefoot and the winner was crowned the Shepherd King. Many steins of beer were drained and everyone had a right knees-up.

In the 1650s the men folk finally deigned to let the women join in and the Shepherdess Race was born. The ladies of Markgröningen were delighted but it seems they took the event a touch too seriously and it frequently descended into an unseemly free-for-all.

'Each wishes of course to win the prize, and, in endeavouring to win it, all means are considered fair,' relates one contemporary report of the race. 'One shoves her companion to make her fall, and will even roll upon the ground with her. Another strikes her neighbour in the side that she may thus, for a time, stop the breath of a dangerous rival.'

In fact, such was the mayhem that the town clerk had to be deployed on horseback to follow the runners, brandishing a whip with which to break up the numerous fights that invariably broke out. The fairer sex it seems were not fair at all.

The contemporary English equivalent of this German festivity was the 'smock race', which was a staple of country fairs the length and breadth of the land from the seventeenth century to the early nineteenth century, and while these events were not renowned for their violence, they were certainly competitive.

As the name suggests, the winner received a smock of fine linen in recognition of her athletic prowess, but from time to time there was another prize on offer in the form of a shiny new husband.

Yes, the local chaps would watch the races and keep an eye out for a potential Mrs Chap. Entry to the races was restricted to young and unwed women – and sometimes being a virgin was also a dubious requirement – and so it seems 'smock races' also served as a bizarre form of rural speed dating at which the menfolk would weigh up the physical attributes of the competitors.

'Maids who wish to be wives can do no better than run for the smock,' urged an article in a contemporary sporting magazine. 'It will afford ample opportunity to demonstrate their strength and pliability when called into action.'

As disturbing as the connotations of 'pliability' are, it is worth remembering these were the days before eHarmony and Match.com, and men and women had to hook up somehow.

ROYAL FREAK SHOW

SUFFOLK, 1660

Sensibilities in the seventeenth century were somewhat different to modern attitudes. After all, back then it was considered perfectly acceptable for girls to get married at the tender age of 12, for men to rub chicken faeces into their heads in a desperate attempt to cure baldness and for communities to execute suspected witches by hanging. As the writer L.P. Hartley famously observed in the opening line of his novel *The Go-Between*, 'The past is a foreign country, they do things differently there.'

It was the same story when it came to running and some of the less edifying athletic events of the century were the so-called 'freak races', which were intermittently staged for the public's dubious pleasure, sad testament to what happens when political correctness is wholly absent.

One of the first documented freak races was staged in 1660 on Newmarket Heath, and among the assembled hordes was none other than King Charles II, fresh from his coronation and the restoration of the monarchy. What unfolded however was scarcely entertainment fit for a king.

'At 3 of the clock in the afternoon,' reported the *The Loyal Protestant* newspaper, 'there was [a] foot race between 2 cripples, each having a wooden leg. They started fair and hobbled a good pace, which caused great admiration and laughter among the beholders, but the taller of the two won by 2 or 3 yards.'

Mercifully the freak races of the eighteenth century that followed this particular spectacle became comical rather than degrading. In 1763, for example, Kennington Common was the scene for a race between a celebrated runner by the name of Isaac Voiterse and a smith called Thomas Dudley. The 'freak' element was provided by the fact Dudley had to make his 100-yard dash on stilts while Voiterse merely had to run, albeit over a longer distance of 120 yards, but our plucky smith still emerged victorious, winning himself a ten-guinea bet in the process.

In the same year, a fishmonger accepted a bizarre running challenge when he agreed to attempt to run from Hyde Park Corner in central London to the 7 mile stone (11.3km away), which stood in Brentford. He had to complete the course in under an hour but he had to do it carrying 55lb (25kg) of fish on his head. If you'll pardon the pun, that's quite a catch, but our purveyor of *fruits de mer* was ultimately triumphant, romping home in just 45 minutes.

Records also suggest that in 1788 there was a race between a young gentleman carrying a jockey on his back, and an elderly fat man by the name of Bullock, but sadly the winner of the unusual contest has been lost in the mists of time.

AGAINST THE CLOCK
BERKSHIRE, 1712

A sundial can make for a charming feature in the garden but they are not exactly the height of precision timing. In short, they're fabulous if you need to know roughly whether it's the morning or afternoon but absolutely bugger all use if you require the ability to accurately measure the passage of time in minutes, let alone seconds.

Which of course made it jolly difficult for our early runners to time themselves. Muttering 'One Mississippi, two Mississippi ...' under their breath wasn't really practical either and the history of running was initially all about who got over the line first. The concept of race times was purely a pipe dream.

The first watches that appeared in Europe in the sixteenth century only had an hour hand, but the inexorable march of technical innovation saw huge strides made in timekeeping, and by the early seventeenth century basic stopwatches had turned up and running would never be quite the same again.

Unsurprisingly the newfangled devices were a big hit on the embryonic athletics scene and timing competitors quickly became all the rage.

One of the first time races on record was an Anglo-Scottish affair staged in 1712, and according to a contemporary account of proceedings by English traveller Celia Fiennes, it was quite the occasion.

'I drove through another part of the Forrest of Windsor to see a race by two footmen an English and Scot,' she wrote. 'The ground measur'd and cut even in a round was almost four miles [6.4km]. They were to run it round so often as to make up 22 miles [35.4km], which was the distance between Chareing Cross and Windsor Cross.

'They ran a round in 25 minutes. I saw them run the first three rounds and halfe another in an hour and 17 minutes. They finish'd it in two hours and a halfe. Many hundred pounds were won and lost about it, they both ran very neatly but my judgement gave it the Scotch man because he seem'd to save himself to the last push.'

The advent of accurate timekeeping has proved seminal in events such as the 100m, where hundredths of a second can be the difference between victory and defeat, but is perhaps not that important if you're an amateur runner who does the occasional 10K. Not that it stops said amateur boring everyone rigid with tales of how they've recently shaved three seconds off their best time. Should you encounter a 'time bore' the best policy is to run away. As quickly as possible.

ROGER'S UNLIKELY RIVAL

LONDON, 1770

It was, depending on who you believe, either Winston Churchill or the early twentieth-century philosopher Walter Benjamin who coined the famous phrase, 'History is written by the victors.' The debate about the origins of the maxim does not concern us here; the point is winners do indeed dictate the narrative that the world inherits, while the losers are quietly airbrushed out of the story.

A case in point in an athletic context is the strange story of the first sub four-minute mile (1.6km). According to the record books of course, it was Sir Roger Bannister who broke the fabled four-minute mark for the first time at a meeting between the British AAA and Oxford University at the Iffley Road Track in 1954, but if we delve further into the annals a surprise rival for the accolade emerges.

Our possible, if seemingly unlikely, history maker is an eighteenth-century fruit and veg man from London by the name of James Parrott. James's athletic background is unknown, but back in 1770 he accepted a wager that he could not run a mile along the streets of the capital in under four-and-a-half minutes. The bet was 15 guineas and JP (as he may or may not have been known to his friends) was up for the challenge.

He absolutely smashed it. In fact, according to the *Sporting Magazine* he was so fleet of foot that he completed the race in record-breaking time. '1770 May 9th,' reported the magazine, 'James Parrott, a coster-monger, ran the length of Old St, viz. from the Charterhouse-wall in Goswell Street, to Shoreditch Church gates, (which is a measured mile) in four minutes.'

So that's that then, James Parrott rather than Sir Roger was the first sub four-minute miler. Well, perhaps. The problem is the *Sporting Magazine* report of his feat was not published until 24 years after the race, casting doubt on its authenticity, and there are also question marks about how accurately the distance of the course was measured.

Sir Roger for one is having one none of it. 'It's inconceivable,' he told the BBC in 2014. 'Without the modern measurement of tracks and stopwatches that are reliable, there was a lot of guesswork in terms of the distance run and I don't think any of these claims are credible.'

Intriguingly there are other historical pretenders to the Bannister throne. In December 1787, the *Oxford Journal* ran a story about a plater from Birmingham called Powell, who accepted a staggering wager of 1,000 guineas to attempt the mile in less than four minutes. There's no record of the race itself but he did apparently clock a time of four minutes and three seconds in a practice run, suggesting he could have done it when it mattered.

In 1796, our old friend the *Sporting Magazine* told the tale of a young athlete by the name of Weller, who 'undertook for a wager of three guineas to run one mile on the Banbury road, in four minutes, which he performed two seconds within the time'.

Sir Roger nearly choked on his cornflakes when he heard about those two possible rivals.

The truth is we'll never know for sure whether Parrott did indeed predate Bannister as the first man to run the mile in under 240 seconds, but for the record, Roger's time in 1954 was three minutes and 59.4 seconds, which was announced inside the stadium by none other than Norris McWhirter, he of *Guinness Book of Records* fame.

'Ladies and gentlemen, here is the result of event nine, the one mile,' Norris intoned over the loud speaker. 'First, number forty-one, R.G. Bannister, Amateur Athletic Association and formerly of Exeter and Merton Colleges, Oxford, with a time which is a new meeting and track record, and which – subject to ratification – will be a new English Native, British National, All-Comers, European, British Empire and World Record.'

Dear Norris didn't get much wrong during his time as the editor of the *Guinness Book of Records* but he may have dropped a clanger there.

RED ROSE RUDENESS

LANCASHIRE, 1824

The proud people of Lancashire are not known for their inclination for frivolity, frippery or even frolicking. The sensible residents of the Red Rose county are content to leave such flamboyant nonsense to 'that lot down south' and focus their energies instead on spreading anti-Yorkshire propaganda and burning effigies of Geoffrey Boycott.

It has not however always been thus, and in the early nineteenth century, it seems Lancashire's finest runners were rather risqué when it came to their choice of race wear. In fact, some just didn't bother at all with the silly social nicety of popping on a pair of pants and sparing everyone's blushes.

The evidence for such a lurid claim comes from a book published in 1873 entitled – you're going to need a deep breath right about now – *Lancashire Legends, Traditions, Pageants, Sports With an Appendix Containing a Rare Tract on the Lancashire Witches.* Not the pithiest title in publishing history perhaps but it does contain some pretty saucy revelations about the lack of modesty, ahem, exhibited by Red Rose runners back in the day.

'During the summer of 1824, I remember seeing at Whitworth in Lancashire two races,' wrote one contributor to the Notes & Queries section of our esteemed literary gem. 'On one occasion two men ran on Whitworth Moor, with only a small cloth or belt round the loins. On the other occasion the runners were six in number, stark naked, the distance being 7 miles [11.3km], or seven times round the moor. There were hundreds, perhaps thousands, of spectators, men and women, and it did not appear to shock them, as being anything out of the ordinary course of things.'

Who'd have ruddy thought it? Lancashire's manliest menfolk casting off their hobnail boots and charging around the countryside in the buff like they just didn't care. Possibly with their hands in the air. The Industrial Revolution has a lot to answer for.

The editor of *Lancashire Legends* (we can take the rest as read), one John Harland, replied thus to the reports of such salacious activity. 'Races by nude men are not yet extinct [in the 1870s] in many parts of Lancashire,' he wrote. 'Notwithstanding the vigilance of the county police.'

Jokes about the vigilance or otherwise of the boys in blue aside, it does raise serious questions about the impact on the crime rate in the Whitworth Moor area at the time if all the bobbies were on the lookout for naked athletes rather than investigating incidents of whippet rustling or inappropriate pigeon fancying.

Contemporary written accounts about nude running in the county begin to disappear around the turn of the century, leading some naïve commentators to misguidedly declare the practice extinct in Lancashire. They have of course never witnessed a well-lubricated stag do in full flight in Blackpool of a Saturday evening.

DEERFOOT IN DEAR OLD BLIGHTY

UK AND IRELAND, 1861

It is an increasingly frequent lament that modern sport lacks characters, idiosyncratic individuals who refuse to play by the rules and don't give a damn if they lose the odd sponsorship deal after indulging in some dubious nocturnal shenanigans, or upset the media by actually expressing an honest opinion. The halcyon days of Beefy Botham, John McEnroe or Seve Ballesteros are sadly gone and we are condemned to live in a grey world in which the expression 'sports personality' is an oxymoron.

Athletics fans of the nineteenth century could make no such complaint when England welcomed one of the most colourful and controversial runners ever to its shores. His name was Deerfoot. Or, in his native tongue, *Hut-goh-so-do-neh*. He also went by the name of Lewis Bennett and sometimes raced as Red Jacket but for the purpose of this tale, we'll stick with Deerfoot.

Our Deerfoot was undeniably a character. A member of the Seneca tribe in North America, he made a name for himself Stateside by winning a few high-profile races, and in 1861 he crossed the Atlantic to embark on a 20-month tour and seek fame and fortune on the vibrant British running scene.

He was a hard man to beat, outstripping Jack 'The Gateshead Clipper' White over 4 miles (6.4km) and Teddy Mills over 10 miles (16.1km) in Dublin among others, and he set the world record for the one-hour race no fewer than four times, but it was his appearance, unique race tactics and penchant for show business, which really marked him out as a crowd-pleaser.

For a start, Deerfoot somewhat scandalised polite society by only running in a skimpy loincloth, his upper torso naked to the elements. Factor in his dark skin and his preference for running in moccasins rather than spikes and you had one of the most exotic sights British athletics had ever clapped eyes on.

He also ran rather unconventionally. Back in those days, a chap was expected to maintain a steady pace over the prescribed distance, but Deerfoot was a maverick and he would delight spectators and infuriate his rivals in equal measure, by overtaking the race leader but then deliberately slowing down. He'd wait for the poor chap to close within a couple of yards and then speed up again, leaving him trailing in his wake. It was cheeky but the fans lapped it up and he would end each race with a terrifying war cry as he crossed the finishing line.

His sense of theatre even extended to a bizarre incident in a bar in Worcester when Deerfoot is said to have lost patience with one of his drinking companions, whipped out a tomahawk, emitted 'a hideous yell' and scalped the poor man. It subsequently emerged the axe was a wooden prop, the scalp a wig and the man a knowing participant in a ruse designed to drum up interest in his next big race.

Sadly the phenomenon could not last forever as his gruelling schedule took its inevitable toll, and after losing badly in what was his final race in England in 1863, he quietly packed his bags and headed home. He died in 1895 but such was his fame that *The New York Times* ran an obituary entitled 'Deerfoot, The Fleet, Is No More'.

Rumours that Kriss Akabusi modelled his career on Deerfoot are true. Possibly.

BOSTON ALMOST GOES
THE DISTANCE
MASSACHUSETTS, USA, 1897

The Tea Party of 1773 and the Celtics. The Freedom Trail and the Red Sox. The city of Boston is famous for many things, but when it comes to the matter of running it's the fabled Boston Marathon that springs to mind, a race with a long and proud history but also has a tendency to somewhat oversell itself.

The state capital of Massachusetts has been staging the race every year since 1897, when it was known rather formally as the Boston Athletic Association Road Race. It is proudly billed as the world's oldest continuous race over the fabled and punishing distance of 26 miles and 385 yards but if we're going to be pedantic here, and let's face it we are, that's not strictly true.

There are two problems with the claim. The first is that the early editions of the Boston Marathons came up short in terms of, well, distance. The course in fact measured a mere 24½ miles (39.4km) back in the day, and it was not until 1924 that the race was finally elongated to 26 miles (41.8km). And a bit.

In its defence, organisers of the Boston Marathon would argue that the marathon at the 1896 Olympics – the inspiration for the race – was run over 24½ miles. That's true M'Lord, but the 1908 marathon at the London Olympics (more of which later) was run over the longer distance, and by 1921 the International Association of

Athletics Federations had set in stone that a marathon was the full monty of 26 miles and 385 yards.

That Boston competitors didn't go all the way, so to speak, until 1924 is all rather embarrassing.

Our second bone of contention is the erroneous claim of continuity since the inaugural event in 1897, because even a quick look at the record books reveals that the race took an unscheduled break in 1918.

The Great War was of course raging and in a move intended to honour American personnel serving in Europe the organisers cancelled the Boston Marathon and replaced it with a military relay race. The new event featured 14 teams from different branches of the Armed Services with ten runners each completing a 2½ mile (4km) stretch.

'It was a departure from the 21 marathon races in previous years,' reported *The Boston Globe* newspaper. 'This year the club, true to its purpose of doing something athletically for our lads in service, abandoned the idea of the time-honored marathon race. The young men of our Army and Navy would find it difficult to secure the time from their daily routine to properly condition themselves for a full race of 25 miles [40.2km].

'It is doubtful, too, if there could have been secured enough full-fledged marathon runners to make a respectable field, and above all else there was the omnipresent horror that a "slacker" might emerge the victor of the historic classic.

'Those sun and wind-bronzed young soldiers and sailors, those deep-chested patriot-athletes had each run 2½ miles at their topmost speed over some part of the historic marathon course from Ashland to Boston, and they did not even breathe deeply.'

So definitely not a 'proper' marathon then. Normal service was resumed the following year, the race being won by a local runner by the name of Carl W.A. Linder, but while the Boston Marathon undoubtedly remains a world-class event and a firm fixture on the athletics calendar, we perhaps need to take some of its historical claims with a pinch of salt.

FRED'S FRAUD EXPOSED

MISSOURI, USA, 1904

'I would prefer even to fail with honour,' observed the Greek dramatist Sophocles, 'than win by cheating.' A fine sentiment indeed, but one which was lamentably lost on our villain of the piece here, the American long distance runner Fred Lorz, in this shameful tale of skulduggery.

The scene is the men's marathon at the 1904 Olympics, the third Games of the modern era, staged in St Louis, Missouri, and Lorz is one of a 32-string field entered in the race. The debilitating 90°F (32.2°C) heat on the day, and a dust bowl of a course, meant only 18 runners successfully completed the race and, when the crowd saw Lorz romping home in first place, there was much general rejoicing. Alice Roosevelt, daughter of incumbent President Theodore, was even on hand to crown Lorz with a laurel wreath but it was then that the muttering started and his triumphant day began to rather unravel.

Lorz had been spotted in the passenger seat of a car for part of the race, which definitely wasn't in the rules, and confronted with his crime he cracked and confessed that for 11 miles (17.7km) of the marathon he'd let the internal combustion engine take the strain. More specifically, he admitted that after 9 miles (14.5km) he'd jumped into his manager's motor and only disembarked when it broke down, running the last 6 or so miles (9.7km) to 'win' the event.

The organisers were absolutely (and understandably) livid and immediately stripped Lorz of his gold medal. The Amateur Athletic Union banned him for life and everybody agreed never to mention his name again. You could almost hear Sophocles turning in his grave.

The strange story of the 1904 Olympic marathon however does not end there. Every race needs a winner and with Lorz's fall from grace complete, the gold medal was awarded to his compatriot Thomas Hicks, who had originally finished 'second' in a time of three hours, 28 minutes and 53 seconds. Which, incidentally, is the slowest time in the event in Games' history.

Hicks though needed some help to complete the race and it later emerged that he had taken performance-enhancing drugs *en route* to victory. 'I decided to inject him with a milligram of sulphate of strychnine and to make him drink a large glass brimming with brandy,' admitted his trainer. 'He set off again as best he could [but] he needed another injection 4 miles [2.5km] from the end to give him a semblance of speed and to get him to the finish.'

Technically strychnine wasn't illegal in the early twentieth century – it has been subsequently banned in athletics – but Hicks certainly couldn't claim to be the cleanest of athletes.

Aside from Lorz's outrageous cheating and Hicks's dubious refuelling, the rest of the 1904 marathon was something of a comedy of errors. The South African runner, Len Tau, was forced to abandon the race after being chased by a pack of wild dogs, while Cuban Felix Carvajal got hungry during the event and stopped in an orchard to snack on some apples. Unfortunately the fruit was rotten and Carvajal was struck down by stomach cramps but he still recovered sufficiently to finish fourth.

The last word though goes to Lorz, who claimed his subterfuge was nothing more than a joke and that he never intended to maintain the deception. He appealed against the ban, it was rescinded on the grounds he was 'temporarily insane' and he went on to win the Boston Marathon in 1905. This time you could definitely hear Sophocles turning in his grave.

GREATNESS IN GLASGOW
GLASGOW, 1904

All athletes dream of breaking world records. To be the fastest man or woman ever on the planet over a given distance is the pinnacle of athletic achievement and, one would imagine, the kudos that comes with such a feat is a great way to get invited to the best parties, hit it off with members of the opposite sex and generally open doors.

Only a select few realise the dream. An even more elite group register multiple milestones on the track, and then we have Alfred 'Alfie' Shrubb, an unassuming long distance runner from Sussex who set a staggering 28 world records in his remarkable career and once, you're going to struggle to believe this, set *seven* new records in a *single* race.

'He was a quiet, working class lad from the rural south of England,' wrote Rob Hadgraft, the author of *The Untold Story of Alfred Shrubb*. 'His hitherto unknown talent for distance-running was discovered one moonlit night, when in his working boots, he raced a horse-drawn fire tender to the scene of a farm fire 3 miles [4.8km] from his home.

'The captain of the local athletics club saw this and immediately invited him to join them. Within a short time Shrubb had become local, then national and then international champion, and was soon amassing titles, trophies and world records. Some of his best times remained unbeaten for almost half a century.

'He was small, wiry and ran like a demon. In his first

big race, in 1900, astonished onlookers labelled him "The Little Wonder", a nickname the press latched on to and which stuck. Within a few years Shrubb's fame had spread worldwide and he laid claim to being athletics' first international superstar.'

A superstar indeed but it was on a November evening in 1904 that our Little Wonder achieved something really very big. The venue was Ibrox Park in Glasgow and Alfie was scheduled to run in an 11 mile (17.7km) race inside the stadium.

He had evidently had his Weetabix that particular day and as he powered past the 6 mile (9.7km) mark in Scotland, the clock confirmed he'd set a new world record for the distance with a time of 29 minutes and 59.4 seconds. He wasn't done yet though and when he completed 10,000m (6¼ miles) in 31 minutes and 2.4 seconds, another record had fallen to Shrubb. It was the same story as he went past seven, eight, nine and 10 miles (11.3, 12.9, 14.5 and 16.1km) and astonishingly it became seven world records when he finished the 11 miles in a time of 56 minutes and 23.4 seconds.

If that's not impressive enough, it's worth noting that Alfie had no pacemakers, let alone speeding fire engines, to help him along in the race and some of his records were not eclipsed until the 1950s.

The Little Wonder hung up his spikes to become the coach of the Harvard University Cross Country team in 1908. A stint as coach of the Oxford University Athletics Club between 1919 and 1928 followed before he immigrated to Canada and lived to the ripe old age of 84.

His feats are commemorated in the village of his birth – Slinfold in West Sussex – with the annual Alf Shrubb Memorial 5 (5 miles/8km), a fitting tribute to one of British athletics' most phenomenal if unheralded competitors.

THE INTOXICATED ITALIAN

LONDON, 1908

It is one of running's golden rules that heavy drinking on the job is rarely a good idea. Just imagine how much you'd spill if you imbibed a bottle of priceless Château Lafite 1787 while stepping out for a brisk 5K ($3^1/_8$ miles) or how many tumbles you'd take after six cans of Special Brew while running cross country.

There's also some other nonsense about rehydration, water and peak physical conditioning, but the salient point here is that the demon drink and running are not a fairytale pairing.

The 1908 Olympic marathon certainly seemed to back up the theory, and it is quite reasonable to suggest had it not been for his love of the liquor, Italy's Dorando Pietri would have been the proud recipient of the gold medal.

One of 75 entrants in the race at the London Games, staged between Windsor Castle and the Great White City Stadium in Shepherd's Bush, Pietri was the first to reach the home straight in front of 75,000 spectators inside the stadium but turned the wrong way onto the track and abruptly collapsed.

The clerk of the course, Jack Andrew, and the chief medical officer, Dr Michael Bulger, helped the Italian to his feet and pointed him in the right direction but Pietri fell a further four times, each time requiring Andrew and Bulger's assistance, and it took him an agonising ten minutes to complete the last 115ft (35m).

Credit where credit's due, he did get over the finishing line first but when American runner-up Johnny Hayes got wind of Pietri's two impromptu helpers, he immediately lodged a complaint. The organisers agreed the Italian had broken the rules that stipulated he must finish the race unaided, he was disqualified and Hayes was the Olympic champion.

At the time many merely assumed the high temperature that day – London was an uncharacteristically balmy 78°F (25.6°C) – and the exertions of the final few miles of the race had done for Pietri, but it wasn't long before there was whispered speculation that his inability to stand up straight was because the Italian was sozzled.

He certainly did nothing to dispel the theory when he spoke to the media about his training methods later in 1908.

'Wine, wine, plenty of wine,' Pietri slurred. 'That's what makes me run. It is so good it keeps me from getting tired. It makes me run long and fast. When I have no wine, I feel faint. It is the liquid of life. After my coffee in the morning, I drink a good Chianti. It wakes me up thoroughly, then I drink some more and go to the running ground. There I drink again. When I feel tired, I call for more wine, and just as soon as I drink I feel new again and continue. When I have run one hour or two hours, and it is sufficient for the day, I drink some more and I am as fresh as when I get out of bed. I drink more at dinner and during the night until I go to bed.'

So quite a big fan of the wine then, our Dorando.

Sober or not, the British public took Pietri to their hearts during the Games, and writing in the *Daily Mail* after the race, the one and only Arthur Conan Doyle no less to took time off from penning Sherlock Holmes' latest adventure to observe that 'the Italian's great performance can never be effaced from our record of sport, be the decision of the judges what it may.'

His 'performance' also earned him the gift of a silver gilded cup presented to him by Queen Alexandra. There are absolutely no prizes for guessing what he immediately poured into it.

INDOORS AT THE ALBERT

LONDON, 1909

Remember our friend Dorando Pietri? The wine-loving marathon runner from Italy? The man who threw away the 1908 Olympic title in London because he'd possibly had one too many? The fella who featured extensively in the previous entry in this very book? Yes, that chap.

Well, Pietri's back and this time is has got absolutely nothing to do with alcohol. No, this time the Italian features because he was part of an unusual marathon which conclusively proved that anything the Yanks can do, the Brits can eventually copy.

The year is 1909 and Pietri is in Blighty. He's just been over in the States after recently accepting a challenge to race against Olympic champion Johnny Hayes in New York in a rematch of their infamous battle at the 1908 Games. The really notable aspect to the race however was the venue – Madison Square Garden – the first time a marathon had ever been staged indoors anywhere in the world.

Not to be outdone by their cousins over the Atlantic, Pietri was invited to England for a repeat performance and in lieu of Madison Square Garden, the Royal Albert Hall was selected. His opponent was local runner C.W. Gardiner and with 19 laps of the famous venue equating to a mile, the lads would have to complete a grand total of 524 laps to clock up the required 26 miles and 365 yards.

The organisers drafted in a military band and an Italian

tenor to entertain the 2,000 spectators lest the sight of two runners lapping a circular track become monotonous and the stage was set for a unique contest.

London however once again proved to be an unhappy hunting ground for the Italian. At the Olympics the previous year it was his alcoholic intake that was to be his downfall while this time it was a mistake of the sartorial variety that was pivotal.

'There was nothing between the men until nearly 12 miles [19.3km] had been run,' reported the *Cycling* magazine. 'When Dorando, who had the lead, suddenly gave way to Gardiner, who passed on the inside and shot ahead, Dorando stopped, and it was discovered that his feet were blistered and raw beyond recovery.

'By some extraordinary piece of bad judgement he had put on a pair of new running shoes and, in consequence, had paid the penalty. He obtained another pair ... but the plucky little Italian had lost his fire and limped badly. The agony he was suffering was shown in his face. He stopped again and rechanged his shoes ... and made another heroic effort to get level ... but it was beyond his powers. He was, to all intents and purposes, crippled.'

And so the first ever indoor marathon in England yielded a home triumph. Gardiner decamped to celebrate with his £100 winner's cheque while Pietri doubtless headed to the nearest wine bar to spend his £50 and drown his sorrows with a nice bottle of Valpolicella.

MISSING IN ACTION
SWEDEN, 1912

If beauty is in the eye of the beholder, what constitutes a good time for the marathon is very much in the eye of the individual runner. Elite athletes are edging inexorably closer to the fabled two-hour mark for the distance while countless amateur runners would be delighted to duck under four hours.

We can all surely agree however that a time of 54 years, eight months, six days, five hours, 32 minutes and 20.3 seconds to complete a single marathon is extremely bloody slow. You could do that distance quicker in a Sinclair C5.

The athlete with the dubious distinction of running such a staggeringly sluggish race is Japanese Shiso Kanakuri and the story of how he took over half a century to cover 26 miles and 365 yards begins at the start line for the marathon at the 1912 Olympics in Stockholm.

It was a big deal for Kanakuri, at the time a 20-year-old student from the Tokyo Higher Normal School, simply to be at the Games. Japan had never before sent athletes to the event and alongside compatriot Yahiko Mishima, he was making history as his country's first ever Olympian.

His race sadly did not go according to plan and after roughly 16 miles (25.7km) Kanakuri collapsed with suspected heat exhaustion. He was found by a kindly Swedish family who took him home, revived him with some raspberry juice and put him to bed. When he awoke a few hours later, he realised the race was over, and embarrassed at his failure to finish, quietly caught a train to Stockholm and then a boat back to Japan.

In fairness there was no shame in not completing the race. Thirty-three other runners from a field of 68 never made it to the finish line that year, but Kanakuri's big mistake was his failure to notify the organisers of his fate, and rather than going into the big book of Olympic records as 'DNF' he was listed as 'missing'.

We must now fast-forward to 1967 when out of the blue Kanakuri, now aged 75, suddenly received an invitation from the Swedish National Olympic Committee asking him to pop back to Scandinavia and officially finish his race. He was, they informed him, famous in the country as the 'missing marathoner' and would he like to return to complete his unfinished business?

He obliged, running a symbolic few final hundred yards (he was after all an OAP by now) and finally breaking the tape in the aforementioned time of 54 years, eight months, six days, five hours, 32 minutes and 20.3 seconds since he first set out. It's a world record many would shy away from but Kanakuri to his credit was philosophical about his milestone. 'It was a long trip,' he told reporters. 'Along the way, I got married, had six children and ten grandchildren.'

A happier footnote to Kanakuri's strange story can be gleaned from the 1920 Olympics when the Japanese athlete returned to marathon action at the Antwerp Games and this time he did finish the race, coming home in a respectable sixteenth place. His time was a positively breakneck two hours and 48 minutes.

LILY'S LONG
TRIP TO THE COAST

LONDON–BRIGHTON, 1923

The pressure on women these days to lose weight immediately after giving birth is a growing and disquieting trend. New mothers who don't shed the unsightly extra pounds within a couple of weeks – and we're not talking about the husband here – are branded slovenly and the rise of the maternal stick insects is as seemingly inexorable as it is unpalatable.

In their desperate quest to become an instant yummy mummy, many women are dusting off their trainers, popping their little bundles of joy into their space-age prams and heading out for a jog. Pushing a pram in front of you while running isn't the easiest form of exercise but, hey, sisters are doing it for themselves. And the fat-shamers on Facebook.

Pram racing however is not actually a new phenomenon and as far back as the early twentieth century, women were ensuring they got some exercise and the kids some fresh air by hitting the roads and running.

The particular race that concerns us here was staged in 1923 and remarkably took place between London and Brighton, a staggering distance of some 52 miles (83.7km). The competitors needed to be up and at them early as the start of the race was at 5.15a.m. on Westminster Bridge.

Contemporary reports of the unusual event in the UK papers are elusive, but it appears the US media couldn't get enough of this quaint British event, and across the Atlantic the American public were regaled with tales of the women's feats.

'Mrs Lily Groom, of Eastbourne, won the Mothers' London-to-Brighton perambulator race today [April 7],' read an article in *The New York Times*. 'She pushed a baby carriage with her two-year-old baby in it a distance of 52 miles in 12 hours 20 minutes. She is 40 years of age and is the mother of five.'

Just imagine how quickly Lily could have completed the course had it not been for all those stops to change nappies and warm up the milk.

So what was the reason for this bizarre race? It was a more innocent time and wasn't in fact a PR stunt conjured up by a pram manufacturer but, according to another American newspaper, the result of a bitter regional rivalry. It was also an event that attracted a certain amount of protest.

'The contest is the outgrowth of a controversy between the mothers of the north and the south of England as to which section had the hardiest and speediest baby carriage chauffeurs,' reported the *Idaho Falls Daily Post*. 'The contestants were cheered by a crowd around the buildings as they got away at dawn on their long trek. They expect to reach Brighton by sunset.

'Officials of the society for the Prevention of Cruelty to Children forwarded a protest against the affair, declaring the performance harmful to the children, and asserting that if the little ones suffered the mothers would be prosecuted. "My baby is in the best of health and temper and I have a bottle of tea at its feet to keep it warm," one of the entrants responded.

'It quickly became apparent that shoe leather and stamina were not the only factors in the race. Mrs Ada May Edwards of Manchester, mother of a five-month-old baby, wheeling a light folding pram, took the lead at the start over the four heavier baby carriages, but soon lost her advance when she had to halt to nurse her offspring who had been loudly voicing its demand for nourishment. It was a quick lunch.

'The pace for the first four hours was so hot that several men accompanying the marching mothers were fatigued on their arrival at Red Hill, but the merry matrons were going strong. The winner will receive a silver "shoving" cup and enough money to buy a pair of shoes.'

It is not clear whether it was compulsory for Lily to buy shoes with her hard-earned winnings but after what was a magnificent demonstration of female stamina, it does seem a tad sexist to suggest she couldn't think of anything else to purchase. And they didn't even sell Manolo Blahniks in those days.

CROSS COUNTRY CHAOS
FRANCE, 1924

Many sports have come and sadly gone in terms of Olympic recognition since the Games were reborn in Athens in 1896. Spectators today can no longer witness the thrills and spills of rope climbing, the days of the whack of leather on willow when cricket was an Olympic event are but a distant memory and we haven't witnessed a gold medal in the tug of war for almost a century.

The noble pursuit of cross country is another sport that has been consigned to the dustbin of Games history, and judging by the absolute chaos in evidence during the last Olympic race in the discipline in Paris in 1924, it really should come as no great surprise.

A total of 38 runners entered the race in 1924. A mere 15 finished and aside from a peerless performance from the eventual winner, Paavo Nurmi of Finland, the day was an utter débâcle.

The searing 104°F (40°C) heat did not help proceedings. A course festooned with waist-high nettles and weeds only exacerbated the problems and the nearby chemical factory belching out thick, acrid smoke was the icing on the cake.

One of the first casualties of the horrendous conditions was Britain's Arthur Sewell, who became so disorientated by it all that he began to run in the wrong direction. A helpful Parisian official kindly pointed him in the right direction but this only proved the catalyst for a nasty collision with another athlete and both men were forced to retire.

The next victim was Spain's Jose Andia, who fell while out on the course, banged his head painfully on a distance marker and started bleeding profusely. At one stage of the race Andia and Edvin Wide of Sweden were actually reported to be dead but mercifully reports of their demise were exaggerated.

There was similar carnage inside the Stade Olympique Yves-du-Manoir and the closing stages of the ill-fated race. The aforementioned Nurmi looked in tip-top shape as he galloped gracefully over the finishing line but his appearance scarcely prepared the spectators for the befuddled condition of the other runners.

Finland's Heikki Liimatainen in particular was all over the place, stopping 98ft (30m) short of the finish convinced his day's work was done. The crowd bellowed to Liimatainen that he'd come up short but he was so exhausted and bewildered it still took him two minutes to complete those last 98ft and finish twelfth.

Rather predictably cross country has not darkened the Olympics' door since the farce that was the race of 1924 although Seb Coe, the recently elected new president of the International Association of Athletics Federations, has gone on record to call for the event's reintroduction. Whether Lord Coe is fully aware of the hilarious trials and tribulations endured by the last participants in the Olympic cross country is unclear.

AN AMERICAN EPIC

USA, 1928

Route 66 is one of the USA's most iconic highways and byways and has been frequently celebrated in popular American culture, lending its name to a 1960s television series and a brand of jeans among others, as well as being immortalised in the seminal hit '(Get Your Kicks On) Route 66', originally recorded by Nat King Cole, but subsequently covered by the likes of The Rolling Stones, Bing Crosby and Depeche Mode.

The fabled motorway opened in 1926 but in the early years the newfangled route from East to West was not an instant hit with fickle American motorists and it was decided a PR stunt of some description was required to generate much-needed publicity for the road.

The idea they hit on was the 'Great American Foot Race', a 3,423 (and a half) mile (5,509km) journey from the Legion Ascot Speedway track in Los Angeles to Madison Square Garden in New York City. Quite why the powers that be believed a sadistically long run was a resonant way to advocate the benefits of driving a car is a moot point but they'd made their minds up and the race was on.

Undeterred by ominous warnings from a leading medical expert, one Dr K.H. Begg, that the race could take five to ten years off the lives of those entered, a total of 199 runners from the age of 16 to 63 signed up. There was after all a hefty $25,000 cheque awaiting the eventual winner and on 4

March 1928 they set off on their epic adventure.

The odyssey was quickly dubbed the 'Bunion Derby' by the American press for obvious reasons and our 199 brave souls certainly had to endure a gruelling schedule, covering 40 miles (64.4km) a day on average. On the seventy-ninth day of the race those still standing had to run an eye-watering 75 miles (121km).

Another problem with the event was the inconvenient fact that it did not always follow the same path as Route 66, which was kind of the point. The race organiser, Charles C. Pyle, was happy to divert proceedings to any town willing to stump up sufficient dollars for the privilege and this meant detours and deviations from the highway were not uncommon.

There were also issues with what we shall kindly call the 'support services'. In reality this was a rudimentary tent city set up at the end of each day, but it often arrived late after the runners had finished, while there were initial rumblings about the sleeping arrangements as competitors from different countries (and, sadly, from different races) refused to bunk down next to each other in the same tent.

The race was won after 12 agonising weeks by Andy Payne, a 20-year-old whippersnapper from Oklahoma, and a member of the Cherokee tribe. He crossed the finishing line in a time of 573 hours, four minutes and 34 seconds, and after collecting his winnings, headed back to Oklahoma and promptly paid off the mortgage on the family farm and built his parents a new house. Bless.

He never ran competitively again. Which doesn't come as a great surprise after his 84-day ordeal on Route 66.

RUMBLE IN THE JUNGLE
TREASURY ISLANDS, 1943

You can invariably tell a military man from his unflappable demeanour, that steely calmness they exude even in the most unforeseen of circumstances. Members of the Armed Forces are just not the sort of chaps to be fazed by stray bullets, explosions or even, God forbid, a Jehovah's Witness at the front door.

Such soldierly stoicism was very much in evidence in the ranks of the New Zealand Army back in 1943, and it's a tale that seamlessly continues our military theme, while at the same time effortlessly interweaving a running element, and it goes something like this.

The Kiwis had just taken the Treasury Islands in the Pacific from the Japanese. The fighting lasted a fortnight, and after driving out the defending Japanese forces, the New Zealanders enjoyed some R&R and decided to organise an athletics carnival to celebrate Christmas and generally give the lads something to do.

On 28 December it was the day of the cross country race through the dense vegetation that covered the islands but things didn't go exactly according to plan. 'The intelligence officer, Lieutenant I.G. Turbott soon went into the lead and held a commanding position to within ½ mile [0.8km] from home,' reports the book *The Third New Zealand Division Histories*. 'At that point he had the disturbing experience of coming upon a Japanese solider at the side of the track.

'He made off into the bush, pursued for a short distance by Lieutenant Turbott, clad in his shorts and jungle boots and, of course, unarmed. Being thus in no condition for a long pursuit, he returned to the track, resumed running and still came in first, to the delight of his several backers who knew of his previous experience in athletic circles in Auckland. On the tote, he returned a handsome figure.'

Now that's pretty impressive composure in the face of the enemy but even Turbott's exploits were eclipsed by one of the other Kiwi soldiers who was trailing behind him in the race.

'The next bunch of runners arrived in with a story of having seen another Japanese soldier on the track at about the same point. Private Keith saw this one in a kneeling position apparently taking aim at one of the leading runners. He threw a piece of coral at him and the man took to his heels.'

The discovery of the two Japanese stragglers during the race was alarming proof the New Zealand invasion was not quite as complete as they first hoped but also that good old Keithy was always a man for a crisis.

DONKEY DERBY

COLORADO, USA, 1949

'Move your ass' is an expression which is familiar to those in the running world. The albeit crude exhortation to quicken one's lacklustre pace is one which many athletes can identify with, particularly at pivotal moments during a race, and it's fair to say that should said athletes succeed in increasing the previously disappointing rapidity of their glutei maximi, their chances of victory will exponentially increase.

In the small American mining town of Fairplay in Colorado however the phrase has an altogether different meaning and brings us neatly to the famed annual 'Burro Days' Festival which was first staged in 1949 and features endurance running with an asinine twist. Asinine in the donkey sense of the word rather than a failure to exercise intelligence or judgement. Or on second thoughts, maybe both.

It's not though donkey racing where the beast does all the work. It's running with an ass – not your own – trotting on a rope behind you. The course is a 29 mile (46.7km) killer, over unforgiving terrain from the foothills of Fairplay up to the 13,000ft (3,963m) summit of the ominous-sounding Mosquito Pass, and on average takes around five hours to complete. Depending of course on the mood of and levels of cooperation afforded to you by your four-legged companion.

The unusual race was created to celebrate Fairplay's gold mining heritage and the ubiquitous use of burros (as the

Americans insist on calling them), and suffice to say the cardinal sin of the event is to take a surreptitious break on the back of your donkey when you think no one is looking.

The first ever 'Burro Days' certainly seemed to capture the imagination in Fairplay and beyond but the sense of excitement was evidently tinged with anxiety as the big day approached.

'In 1949 when the challenge went out to anyone with the fortitude to race from Leadville to Fairplay for a $500 prize,' relates the race website, 'every mountain town in the Rockies came alive in the following weeks trying to lure racers into representing them. Mosquito Pass became a mecca for aspiring racers. The local bars reported that those runners consuming more beer were producing faster practice times. The Fairplay Flume reported that there were more burros escaping from their pasture than ever remembered.

'There were weekly reports of the status of Fairplay's local racer Ed Knizely and the whereabouts of his burro, Prunes IV. A lot of local money was backing this team, so the town was on alert about the escape tactics of Prunes.

'On race day 21 entrants showed up for the start. After a hectic start a racer from Como, Melville Sutton, took the lead and was the first to the top of the pass. The trip down the pass had local favorite Ed Knizely battling for the lead with Melville Sutton. In Park City, Sutton pulled ahead after the course finally took its toll on Knizely's knees and feet.'

The 1960s however witnessed some of the most fiercely contested 'Burro Days' as out-of-towners with silly shorts, fancy trainers and pedometers (did they have those in the 1960s?) attempted to gatecrash the party and beat the miners at their own game. The local hero was Joe Glavineck and although he may have lacked a certain finesse in his running style, his Dolittle-esque ability to speak to the animals was his trump card.

'He had some kind of special rapport with his burros that

kept him in first place for over 20 years. His battles with marathoner Steve Matthews became legendary, showing that it takes more than being a good runner to win this race. Glavenick was the last of the true miners to win the race, but he beat the best runners of the time including some Olympic hopefuls who took the challenge.'

The 'Burro Days' Festival endures to this day and proudly goes by the tagline 'Get your ass up the pass'. 'Drag a stubborn donkey up a mountain' doesn't after all have quite the same ring to it.

AND THE
BAND PLAYED ON ...
FINLAND, 1952

Without wishing to sound unkind, Luxembourg doesn't exactly boast a multitude of claims to fame. It's a jolly nice country of course (lovely architecture, spectacular countryside, rich history, that sort of thing) but it's never going to be first on the list if Europe decides to stage a big party and everyone's invited. That's Germany obviously.

That said, and despite its modest population of just 540,000 (putting it on a personnel par with the whole of Sheffield), Luxembourg can proudly point to the fact it has produced an Olympic gold medallist. Which is one in the eye for the likes of Afghanistan, Ghana and Kuwait to name but three.

Our Luxembourgian hero is middle distance runner Josy Barthel. His date with destiny came in 1952 at the Games in Finland and his story is one which begins with one of the biggest shocks in Olympic history and ends in farce and tears. We shall explore whether the blubbing was down to joy or embarrassment in due course.

Barthel was principally a 1500m runner. He had finished ninth over the distance in the 1948 Olympics in London, but four years later he travelled to Helsinki as the proverbial underdog, trailing in the betting behind the likes of Germany's Rolf Lammers, Denis Johannson of Finland and the American Robert McMillen. There was also a yet-to-be-anointed Sir Roger Bannister in the field.

Our man battled his way through to the final but for much of the race was behind, only to make his devastating move in the last straight, speeding past German world record holder Werner Leug and then holding off the challenge of McMillen. As he triumphantly crossed the finishing line, Luxembourg had its first, and to date only, Olympic champion.

The problem was no one, least of all the Finnish Games organisers, had expected Barthel to win. The band charged with playing the national anthems during the medal ceremony were bereft of the sheet music for the Luxembourg anthem, and when Barthel proudly mounted the podium, the assembled musicians were hastily forced to improvise. There is an iconic picture of Barthel on the podium, his fingers pressed firmly against moist eyes, but to this day we still do not know whether his tears were the result of sheer joy or despair at the orchestra's pained attempts to recreate his country's national song. It was, after all, the only time the tune had (or has) been heard at the Olympics.

Interestingly, Barthel's status as Luxembourg's only Olympic champion subsequently came under some scrutiny when it emerged that 'French' marathon runner Michel Theato, the champion at the 1900 Games in Paris, was actually born in Luxembourg. The International Olympic Committee still recognise Theato's win as a French victory, but should they ever reverse their decision, it would surely be enough to drive Barthel to tears once again.

HOGAN'S HEAD SLAM

LONDON, 1960s

The adulation that accompanies victory in a major championship is what all elite athletes aspire to, but like runners of all abilities, they must endure the indignities and potential hazards that come with hours of training. Everyone has to put in the hard and frequently painful yards.

James 'Jim' Hogan won gold in the marathon for Great Britain at the 1966 European Championships in Budapest. He ran at the 1964 and 1968 Olympic Games and was, by anyone's measure, a high-quality athlete. Judging by this tale, however, he was just as susceptible to an unglamorous mishap as any of us mere mortals.

Jim was out on a training run with the famed Dave Bedford (more of whom shortly) in Teddington in south-west London one day. The pair's pace was brisk and as they crossed a footbridge and set off down a hill, Bedford was marginally in front. Bedford naturally was focused on his form and with only seconds to spare noticed a protruding sign overhanging their route and jerked his head out of the way to avoid a nasty injury. Sadly he didn't have time to warn his partner of the impending danger, and Hogan ran full square into it, knocking himself unconscious.

Two worrying minutes passed as the future European marathon champion lay prostrate and motionless and Bedford had not a clue what to do. If only they had invented mobile phones a hasty call to 999 could have been made. Mercifully Hogan made a Lazarus-like recovery just as Bedford was mentally composing his eulogy but it was evident that the former was blissfully unaware of the extent of his misadventure as he dusted himself off and continued his run.

'You were out cold for two minutes,' Bedford informed him.

'I never was,' Hogan replied. 'I just tripped over for a moment.'

Bedford's own career burned brightest in the 1970s, setting a world record for the 10,000m in 1973 and competing in the Munich Olympics the year before, but his standalone place in this book is earned courtesy of his bizarre and rather last-gasp decision to run in the 1981 London Marathon.

It was the night before the big race. Dave was in the nightclub in Luton, the Mad Hatter, which he owned, when he was approached by a punter who bet him £250 he couldn't run the marathon. Now Dave didn't get where he is today by turning down a challenge, and the wager was defiantly accepted after he had called up race organiser Chris Brasher, and asked for a cheeky late entry number.

Sorted. The only problem was Dave didn't exactly hasten to his bed in preparation for his impending 26 miles and a bit. In fact, it was only after four piña coladas, a pint and a dubious prawn curry that he finally hit the sack at quarter to five in the morning, and unsurprisingly his pre-race preparation would ultimately take its toll.

Amazingly he did finish but along the way the booze and his sumptuous late-night banquet demanded to make an urgent reappearance as he was forced to pull over and 'lighten his load'. 'I only decided the night before and I had been drinking,' he admitted. 'I was on all fours, leaning over a manhole cover being sick, losing the rest of the curry into a drain and on the Beeb, Brendan Foster says, "There's Dave Bedford looking, er, not quite as fit as we might have expected." It took me 45 minutes to run the last 3 miles [4.8km].'

Quite. Later in life Bedford served as the race director for the London Marathon and unsurprisingly during his tenure 'cocktails and curry' did not feature under helpful tips for prospective runners.

WHAT'S IN A NAME?
MASSACHUSETTS, USA, 1967

'Women can't run in the Marathon,' raged race director Will Cloney after the conclusion of the 1967 Boston Marathon. 'The rules forbid it. Unless we have rules, society will be in chaos. I don't make the rules, but I try to carry them out. We have no space in the Marathon for any unauthorized person, even a man. If that girl were my daughter, I would spank her.'

Controversial to say the least. Threats of corporal punishment are never particularly palatable but it is Cloney's undisguised athletic misogyny which concerns us here.

The subject of Will's wrath was a pioneering lady by the name of Kathy Switzer and her place in running history was cemented in Boston in the 1960s when, whether unwittingly or not, she gatecrashed the marathon, a race in those less enlightened times which was still the exclusive preserve of men, but one which Kathy managed to register for and, crucially, receive an official race number.

How she did this however was neither cunning nor covert, she simply applied to run and put pen to paper on the dotted line. 'I filled in my Amateur Athletic Union number and plunked down $3 cash as entry fee,' she wrote in her memoir *Marathon Woman*. 'I signed as I always sign my name, "K.V. Switzer" and went to the university infirmary to get a fitness certificate.'

Cloney and Co. evidently didn't blink an eye, erroneously assuming K.V. Switzer was a fella, and come the big day Kathy, her boyfriend and a few friends headed to Boston and the starting line. The rest of the field of course noticed that she wasn't in fact a he but none of the organisers by this stage had learned of the impending scandal. 'As runners jogged past, most kept their nervous eyes ahead, lost in prerace concentration,' she wrote, 'but plenty did double takes, and when they did I'd smile back or wave a little wave. Yep, I'm a girl, my look back said.'

Up to the 4 mile (6.4km) mark things were going swimmingly but that all changed when a race official called Jock Semple spotted Kathy and got quite cross. In fact he was bloody furious and waded into the runners with the express intention of executing an immediate expulsion.

'A man with an overcoat and felt hat was then in the middle of the road shaking his finger at me,' she said. 'He said something to me as I passed and reached out for my hand, catching my glove instead and pulling it off. I did a kind of stutter step, we all had to jostle around him. I thought he was a nutty spectator, but when I passed I caught a glimpse of a blue and gold BAA ribbon on his lapel.

'A big man, a huge man, with bared teeth was set to pounce, and before I could react he grabbed my shoulder and flung me back, screaming, "Get the hell out of my race and give me those numbers!" Then he swiped down my front, trying to rip off my bib number, just as I leapt backward from him. He missed the numbers, but I was so surprised and frightened that I slightly wet my pants and turned to run.'

Now Semple may have been a big man but he wasn't as big as Kathy's boyfriend, who just happened to be a 17st (108kg) ex-American footballer and hammer thrower, and Big Tom Miller (that's honestly his name) took rather spectacular exception to his girlfriend being manhandled.

'A flash of orange flew past and hit Jock with a cross-body block. It was Big Tom, in the orange Syracuse sweatshirt.

There was a thud – whoomph! – and Jock was airborne. He landed on the roadside like a pile of wrinkled clothes. Now I felt terror. We've killed this guy Jock. It's my fault, even though hothead Tom did it. My God, we're all going to jail.'

Kathy or for that matter Big Tom didn't end up in Sing Sing. She finished the marathon in four hours and 20 minutes, and although it would take a further five years for the Boston Athletic Association to finally see the light and officially welcome female runners, Kathy's contribution to the cause ultimately changed the gender equation forever.

THE SUDHAUS SCANDAL
GERMANY, 1972

One of the highlights for the winner of any marathon is surely that feeling they get as they complete the final few hundred yards of the course to a cacophony of cheering and roars from the crowd, the wall of noise that signals the end of their endeavours and the admiration of the assembled spectators.

Spare a thought then for American Frank Shorter who was greeted by a chorus of boos and caterwauling as he entered the Olympic Stadium in Munich *en route* to collecting the marathon gold medal at the Games in 1972. Given that Shorter was born in Germany before his family moved back to the USA, it was probably not the reception he'd been expecting and there wasn't even a German runner close to him, rendering the loud Teutonic ire of the 72,000 spectators a complete mystery.

What Frank didn't know was that moments before he made what he had hoped would be a triumphant entrance inside the stadium, a young German 'athlete' by the name of Norbert Sudhaus had already hit the home straight, and initially the crowd were ecstatic at the prospect of crowning a homegrown champion.

But Sudhaus was not all he seemed. He had a German team running vest, some nice running shoes and a rather fetching pair of shorts. His blonde mop of hair was to die for but as he jogged around the track of the Olympic Stadium, seasoned athletic observers began to smell a rat.

'Now here's something, this is, this is very puzzling,' stuttered the BBC's commentator. 'This man is not on the programme. It's a hoax. It's somebody having a lark. I don't think it's a demonstration, but he looks as fresh as a buttercup.' The American commentator for ABC, Erich Segal (who incidentally was the man who wrote *Love Story*), was a little more direct. 'That is an impostor,' he screamed. 'Get him off the track! This happens in bush league marathons! Throw the bum out! Get rid of that guy!'

Which is exactly what happened as security guys unceremoniously bundled Sudhaus off the track and out of the stadium, no doubt for some serious interrogation. The coast was clear for Shorter and he romped home in first place, although it only became clear to him after he had finished that the crowd were venting their spleen at Sudhaus's antics rather than him.

To paraphrase Scooby Doo, Sudhaus may very well have got away with it if it hadn't have been for his pesky running vest. It was authentic issue all right, but it didn't have a race number pinned to it, and it was this fatal flaw in his plan that proved his undoing. We're still not exactly sure why he did it but the most popular theory is it was nothing more than a stupid bet.

Shorter retired to the athletes' village after his victory and apparently celebrated with three large gins while soaking in a hot bath. Rather ominously, Sudhaus has not been heard of since.

PETER'S ROAD RAGE
SOUTH YORKSHIRE, 1973

A keen, innate sense of direction is an important attribute in a runner. It can preclude all manner of inadvertent mishaps, ranging from the embarrassment of getting lost *en route* to the start line, to finishing up in Scarborough rather than South Shields while taking part in the Great North Run. It is all relative however and, as this story underlines, a runner's ability to head in the right direction is meaningless if the race organisers don't know what the hell they're doing.

The victim of our tale of administrative misadventure is none other than Peter Elliott, the 1990 Commonwealth Games gold medallist in the 1500m, and the runner-up over the same distance at the Olympics in Seoul two years earlier. This vignette however is focused on Peter's early years and his embryonic cross country career at Rawmarsh Community School in South Yorkshire.

It is the day of the district championships. After initially trailing the leaders, Elliott surges in front on the 1 mile (0.8km) mark when he encounters a schoolboy marshal who confidently informs him and the chasing pack of the route they need to follow. 'Over the fence,' is the instruction, 'down the bank and left along the road.'

'As we turned left and headed up the road, I glanced anxiously back and realised that I had managed to increase my lead and it was a group of just four or five boys that were leading the chase about 50m [164ft] behind,' Elliott recalls in the book *Funny Running Shorts*. 'I put my head down and ran for all I was worth.'

Elliott never made it to the finishing line, interrupted as he was by the sudden wail of sirens, and the wholly unexpected sight of a police car pulling up alongside him. 'Get in,' shouted the long arm of the law. 'You must be joking,' replied Elliott. 'I'm in the middle of a race and I'm in the lead.' The boys in blue were having none of it though and Elliott was unceremoniously bundled into the back of the car and his race was prematurely over.

Seething after being robbed of his chance of victory, Elliott politely enquired to the nature of his crime. 'You can't run down this road,' replied the officer. 'It's the M1.'

Quite how the young Elliott failed to notice six lanes of traffic speeding past him at 70mph (113km/h) is admittedly a moot point, but the bulk of the blame must rest with our young marshal, who was unsurprisingly conspicuous by his absence when Elliott returned to the course to have a 'quiet word'.

THERE'S A MOOSE LOOSE!

NORWAY, 1970s

The litany of bizarre injuries sustained by footballers over the years is as long as it is funny. The players of the beautiful game are, it seems, past masters at nobbling themselves in repeatedly unusual and embarrassing ways and their mishaps are enough to make any manager weep.

England international Rio Ferdinand once strained a knee tendon while playing Xbox. Goalkeeper Dave Beasant fell foul of salad cream when he dropped a bottle of the stuff on his big toe, while fellow custodian Alex Stepney once dislocated his jaw after shouting too vigorously instructions to his Manchester United team-mates. A Croatian player by the name of Milan Rapaic once sidelined himself after inexplicably thrusting his plane boarding pass into his eye. Why some people don't believe footballers are Mensa material is a mystery.

The daddy of all surreal football injuries however occurred in the 1970s, and in case you have started to wonder when running was going to make an overdue reappearance in the narrative, it centres on a player out for a morning jog. We'll call the player Svein Grondalen, mainly because that's his name, and back in the 1970s he was an international footballer for Norway, a tough-tackling defender, noted for his rugged style of play.

Svein liked to jog to build his stamina, but on the fateful morning in question he got rather more than he bargained for on his run through the forest, when he had a contretemps with a bloody great big moose and sustained a nasty gash to his leg.

The exact details of his unfortunate encounter with the moose have been distorted in the retelling over the decades. One version of the story is that Svein literally stumbled over the sleeping beast and cut his leg as he fell. Another contends he awoke the moose, who wasn't happy at having his 40 winks interrupted, and charged our unfortunate footballer who was forced to take evasive action and leap off the edge of a steep incline in order to escape. Another take on the tale is that Svein simply ran into the animal and came off worst.

The upshot of the incident was a serious cut, which required stitches, and ruled Svein out of an important upcoming World Cup qualifying match. Oh to have been a fly on the office wall as he informed an incredulous Norway manager exactly why he was unable to play.

'PULLING A ROSIE'
NEW YORK, USA, 1980

Fame can be fleeting or fame can last. It's a fickle mistress and it is only through the prism of time that an individual and their achievements can be properly judged and we can assess whether their legacy has endured or they've cruelly been consigned to the 'here today, gone tomorrow' category.

Infamy on the other hand is a stubborn bugger. Everyone remembers the villains, don't they? Take the women's Olympic 3,000m in Los Angeles, for example. We all remember little Zola Budd tripping up the home favourite Mary Decker in the final but can you name the winner of the race? It was a Romanian called Maricica Puică if you're interested.

The point is notoriety lingers, and to prove it we shall now explore the nefarious exploits of American marathoner Rosie Ruiz, a woman whose name still resonates in running circles over in the States. For all the wrong reasons.

Her story begins in 1979 when she entered the New York City Marathon and came home in eleventh place in the women's race in two hours, 56 minutes and 29 seconds. Her time was good enough to qualify her for the Boston Marathon the following year, and Ruiz proceeded to run a scorching two hour, 31 minute and 56 second race, as she crossed the line ahead of all other female entrants.

'Miss Ruiz, an administrative assistant for Metal Trading Inc. in Manhattan, received the traditional laurel wreath, a medal and a silver bowl for her victory,' reported *The New York Times*. 'But as late as three hours after she had been interviewed by newsmen and photographed with [men's winner Bill] Rodgers, Will Cloney, the race director, acknowledged that "there is an obvious problem with the determination of the women's winner".

'Later [that] evening, during an interview in her hotel room, Miss Ruiz, noticeably shaken by the unexpected attention thrust upon her, insisted, "I ran the race. I really did … When I got up this morning, I had so much energy." Miss Ruiz said she was prepared to take a lie-detector test. "I would take anything," she said. "I don't want to cause a commotion."'

A 'commotion' was putting it mildly. It was a nationwide scandal and despite lacking absolutely incontrovertible evidence that she had cheated in some way, four days later the Boston Athletic Association officially disqualified Ruiz and installed Canadian Jacqueline Gareau as the champion.

It was of course an era before wall-to-wall CCTV so there was no photographic proof of Ruiz hailing a cab during the race, jumping on a train or even mounting a motorcycle, but the race organisers, other competitors and the public had no doubt she was a fraud.

The weight of evidence against her was crushing. She wasn't sweating or breathing heavily when she crossed the line. Her 25-minute improvement on her time from the New York Marathon was simply unprecedented and other runners and race officials could not remember seeing her for vast swathes of the race. Tests showed her resting heart rate was 76 rather than the average 50 for most female marathoners, she could not remember long stretches of the course when quizzed, while two Harvard students told a tale of seeing Ruiz burst from a crowd of spectators about ½ mile (0.8km) from the finish line.

It would take Rumpole of the Bailey on steroids to get her off this one.

The most damning evidence was yet to come however, and was offered by a freelance photographer called Susan Morrow, who recognised Ruiz in all the furore after the race and came forward to relate a hugely incriminating story. Morrow it emerged had met Ruiz on the subway *during* the running of the New York Marathon the previous year. Ruiz had told her she was an injured runner *en route* to the race HQ to inform the organisers she could not complete the course, but she was erroneously marked down as a finisher and given an impressive time, which in turn booked her place in Boston.

She did nothing to correct the error and as The Sweeney might have observed, she obviously had 'form'.

Ruiz never revealed how she did it but life certainly went downhill for her after Boston. In 1982 she was arrested for embezzling money from the real estate company she worked for and she had her collar felt again the following year for conspiracy to supply cocaine.

Her notoriety shows no signs of abating. Every year a bar in Boston, a mile (1.6km) from the finish of the marathon course, unfurls a banner declaring 'Rosie Ruiz starts here' while 'pulling a Rosie' remains American slang for cheating. As Kenneth Williams famously quipped in *Carry On Cleo*, 'Infamy, infamy, they've all got it in for me.'

TREADING A TECHNOLOGICAL PATH

GERMANY, 1984

The year 1984 was a significant one in the world of technology and computing. Over in the US of A our American cousins were rioting to get their hands on Apple's first ever Macintosh (blissfully oblivious to the fact it was the start of an enduring global addiction to absolutely anything emblazoned with the company's fruity logo), while Phillips introduced the world's first ever CD-ROM.

Over in Blighty we had to be satisfied with plucky Clive Sinclair's offering of the ZX Spectrum+ (which at least mercifully boasted a better keyboard than the old, iconic Spectrum), while in Japan a clever chap and Toshiba employee called Fujio Masuoka invented flash memory.

Heady technological times indeed, and an innovative wave which runners were also able to ride that year when Adidas joined the fray with the release of their 'Micropacer' trainer, the world's first athletic footwear (or shoe of any kind) to incorporate a computer.

The Micropacer boasted a sensor placed under the big toe, which was triggered when the jogger pushed off the ground, and the teeny-weeny computer (it was, after all, 1984) to which it was attached would then calculate distance travelled, average pace and calories burned.

Adidas of course insisted the product would be at the vanguard of a new generation of 'intelligent trainers' (and increased profits), and although you can still buy pairs of

Micropacers today, it was not quite the hit they hoped for. Not least because they hadn't fully anticipated the damage done to the circuitry when runners inadvertently stepped in ruddy great puddles.

Adidas picked up the computing baton again in 2005, when they proudly released their Adidas-1 trainers, which featured a computer buried in the heel and measured levels of compression each time the sole hit the deck. The microprocessor would then send a signal to a small, motor-driven cable system that changed the shape and cushioning level of the trainer depending on the nature of the terrain. Running on hard tarmac would result in a slackening of the cables to give more cushioning while a quick jog on lovely soft grass would see the system stiffen up.

That was the theory at least. Adidas were rather pleased with what they claimed was a mere 25-millisecond delay between their gizmo receiving data and the system making the changes and claimed the battery lasted for 100 hours. Which is a lot of running in anyone's book.

'We definitely believe,' the head of the Adidas development team Stephen Pierpoint insisted, 'there is a true athlete benefit of using these shoes.' Well he would say that, wouldn't he? In reality though Adidas-1 were probably too intricate for their own good and many pairs spent more time in the repair shop than they did out on the road. As a result they are now no more than a, well, footnote in running history.

What the future holds for digital trainers is hard to predict, but a pair capable of simultaneously sending emails, ordering the weekly shop from Sainsbury's online and allowing you to play Candy Crush while jogging remain some way off yet.

WHEELS OF MISFORTUNE
CALIFORNIA, USA, 1985

Runners have a multitude of potential enemies. Dogs are obviously a staple threat, pavements thronged with OAPs outside the Post Office waiting to collect their pensions are an accident waiting to happen, while many an amateur athlete has fallen foul of the runners' ultimate nemesis, the evil Nazi diamond hunter. Oh hang on, that's Laurence Olivier in *Marathon Man*, isn't it?

Anyway the salient point here is that runners need to have eyes in the backs of their heads to stay safe, but sadly in the case of British athlete Steve Anders, his 360-degree vision rather let him down in the 1980s when he was over in the USA to compete in the annual Superbowl 10K in Los Angeles.

To begin with the race was all tickety-boo for our Steve and by the halfway point – that's 5km/3^1/$_8$ miles for the 'mathematically challenged' among you – he was as happy as Larry nestled as he was in the small leading group of runners.

At this point the leaders passed a wheelchair racer who evidently made quite an impression. 'This guy was certainly not an ordinary sight,' said Steve. 'He had spray painted the whole of his machine jet black, he was wearing black leather trousers and had a dark visor. He certainly looked the business.' It was not long however before Anders' admiration for this vision in black had turned to consternation as he made an altogether different impression on him.

The leading group headed up a steep hill, leaving their new chum in their wake. The incline eventually levelled off and they were heading downwards and preparing for a sharp right-hand turn, when the wheelchair racer suddenly renewed acquaintances after picking up an alarming amount of speed, thanks to the powerful effects of gravity.

He made to turn right but such was his velocity that he misjudged the manoeuvre badly and one of the leading group found themselves coming off worse in an unscheduled head-to-head with the wheelchair.

'Unfortunately that runner was me,' admitted Steve, in a revelation that surprised absolutely no one. 'I went down like a bag of spuds with elbows and knees grazed and knees banged up. Badly bruised on my left side, I got up and managed to complete the race but the most embarrassing thing of all was returning to the UK and explaining that I had finished in a lowly seventh place as a result of being run over by a wheelchair.'

The fate of the wayward wheelchair racer is unknown but it's probably safe to assume he avoided arrest for failure to stop at the scene of an accident.

BOOZE ON THE RUN
WISCONSIN, USA, 1987

Most runners wait until the end of a race before popping a celebratory cork and enjoying a little liquid refreshment, but for 25 glorious years entrants in the 'Beer Belly Two' event near Green Bay in the USA would happily imbibe alcohol as they ran the 2 mile (3.2km) course.

As the name subtly suggests, beer was the tipple of choice for the race, and ever since the inaugural event in 1987 competitors have been required to stop at four drink stations along the way and partake of the amber nectar, while root beer was provided for those under the age of 21. It's a crazy country in which you can buy a gun in some states at the age of 18 but you have to wait three more years to legally enjoy a cold one. Probably a debate for another day though.

The 'Beer Belly Two' may not have exactly been the pinnacle of athletic prowess but it was jolly popular with the locals. 'This way the wife allows me to have a couple of beers because you're doing something,' enthused one race veteran. 'A little exercise, you kill two birds with one stone.'

Sadly the 'Beer Belly Two' ceased to be after the 2012 race amid unsubstantiated reports that the event's amply proportioned competitors were causing too much damage to the local roads, and stories of fights frequently breaking out over who spilled whose pint, but the spirit (if you'll excuse the unintended pun) of alcohol-fuelled, fun-filled racing lives on.

One of the most famous examples is Le Marathon du Medoc, held every year in September around Pauillac near Bordeaux, and it is the epitome of a party event as runners resplendent in their fancy dress negotiate a 26 mile (42km) course which conveniently takes them past a number of chateaux where they can indulge in the finest French delicacies. And wine. Lots of lovely wine.

Runners are given six hours to finish the race and it's an extremely popular event. So popular in fact that in 2014 organisers had to reject 40,000 applications from hopeful runners. 'If we had accepted all requests, this would be the biggest marathon in the world,' boasted marathon grand fromage Albert Duvocelle. It's all the wine, Albert, the lovely French wine.

Journalist Vicky Lane was one of the lucky ones to get the green light for the 2014 instalment of Le Marathon du Medoc and her experience encapsulated what the race is all about.

'This marathon – to the organisers' pride – has the most medical support of any in the world, not that it seems to need it,' she wrote in *The Guardian*. 'Unlike in the London and Paris Marathons I only saw one floored person (a Smurf, surprise surprise) on the entire route.

'Maybe it's because there is less pressure to run fast or maybe I was just too drunk to notice. When we finally stumble over the finish line, sunburnt and tipsy, we're happy. Until we realise that we have taken six hours and 52 minutes. What the hell happened?'

WHAT PRICE SUCCESS?

SWITZERLAND, 1989

A report in the *Financial Times* in February 2014 revealed a startling economic trend in Britain, namely that 40 per cent of all household credit card debt in the UK could be directly attributed to the impulse purchase of expensive trainers. OK, that's completely made up, but I had you going there for a moment.

The point is that trainers, or more specifically running shoes, are astronomically expensive. In 2015, for example (and this is not fabricated for illustrative purposes), a pair of Asics GEL-KINSEI 5 would set you back £165, while some lovely new Nike Flyknit Air Max were a bargain at £180. Alternatively, for £220 of your hard-earned cash, you could treat yourself to a pair of Adidas Ultra Boost Shoes designed by, wait for it, that well-known athlete and Hampstead Fun Run champion of 1981, Stella McCartney.

But you get what you pay for, right? Well perhaps not if we are to believe a seminal study published in 1989 that rather upset the likes of Adidas, Nike *et al* and might just lead you to reassess whether those new bright yellow 'Mega-Mile Pro9000 Enduro-Flyers' (and that is definitely made up in the interests of avoiding litigation) are really worth selling a kidney for.

The study in question was conducted by Dr Bernard Marti of the University of Bern in Switzerland. His research team asked 4,358 runners who competed in the Bern Grand

Prix, an annual 10 mile (16.1km) road race, to complete an extensive questionnaire about their training regimes, their injury history and the shoes they wore, and when all the data was dissected and analysed, Marti made a startling discovery. Specifically the good doctor found that runners wearing high-end trainers were 123 per cent more likely to get injured than counterparts wearing cheap footwear. He also concluded that runners in shoes that cost more than $95 were twice as likely to nobble themselves as those who had spent $40 or less on their footwear.

The respective share prices of the leading trainer manufacturers fell quicker than a hungover jogger on a frosty morning.

The thing is Dr Marti (who narrowly escaped the clutches of the assassin Nike sent to silence him) is not the only one to suggest that top-of-the range trainers are not all their price tags suggest they should be. 'Wearers of expensive running shoes that are promoted as having additional features that protect (e.g. more cushioning) are injured significantly more frequently than runners wearing inexpensive shoes,' argued a study published in 1991 in *Medicine & Science in Sports & Exercise*.

In 2008, a paper for the *British Journal of Sports Medicine* by Dr Craig Richards of the University of Newcastle (the one in Australia rather than the north-east of England), asserted that there was no evidence whatsoever that running shoes made athletes less prone to injury compared to going barefoot, and the following year journalist-cum-runner Christopher McDougall published a book, *Born to Run*, in which he claimed jogging *sans* shoes was far better for the body.

'When the book came out, I assumed that the collective ire of the podiatrist community would unite against me,' McDougall told *The Independent* in an interview in 2009. 'But I am hearing from more and more podiatrists every week who want to talk about the benefits of barefoot running. It's interesting because I've put out a challenge to the training-shoe industry to show me one study that their products aren't causing damage and they haven't yet. I keep on getting emails from people saying they have got back the use of their legs for the first time in years. The excitement it has generated has been overwhelming.'

So should you ditch the trainers and let the grass kiss your feet while you're next out training? With the global market for trainers estimated to be worth somewhere north of $20 billion per year (which is more than enough to pay for an army of litigation lawyers), all those associated with this humble book couldn't possibly comment.

A SHADY EXIT IN SPLIT
YUGOSLAVIA, 1990

By the nature of their discipline, marathoners are probably running's unluckiest group. When you spend hours upon hours out on courses that aren't really courses at all, you're going to be vulnerable to the slings and arrows of outrageous misfortune, and a lot can potentially go wrong before the long distance runner has safely completed those arduous 26 miles and 385 yards.

This is why marathoners are disproportionally represented in tales of athletic woe. They are running's equivalent of sacrificial lambs, callously despatched to hazard-strewn city streets and uncharted, desolate rural roads with only a sweatband for protection, and it's a miracle so many of them actually make it back alive.

The men's marathon at the 1990 European Championships in Split, in what was formerly Yugoslavia, now Croatia, claimed another victim. But it did so in highly comical fashion so let's all have a laugh at another hapless athlete's misfortune.

The race was around 3 miles (5km) old and with the mercury tipping over 80°F (27°C), the runners were eagerly anticipating arriving at the first drinks station. What they weren't expecting was the wet sponge station sited just before it, and as the leading group arrived the first two runners grabbed for a sponge, but in the process contrived to accidentally tip over the table.

This was bad news for contestant number three who suddenly found his way blocked by an upturned table, a slew of wet sponges and an umbrella, which had been thoughtfully positioned at the station to provide some, albeit fleeting, shade for the runners. Unfortunately his attempts to avoid the unscheduled obstacle did not go well.

'By some extraordinary feat of gymnastics, in attempting to get out of the way, he succeeded only in getting one leg either side of the parasol system,' wrote Geoff Wightman, who finished sixth in the race and recorded the mishap for prosperity in *Funny Running Shorts*. 'In this ungainly, straddling manner he was unable to stop himself from plunging right into the canopy of the parasol.

'He let out a loud curse. My last sighting of him was as his fall triggered the release of the mechanism and the canopy began to close round him like some sort of giant Venus fly trap.'

Undone by an umbrella. It's a hell of a way to bow out and further proof that there's danger lurking everywhere for the intrepid breed that is the marathon runner.

LET'S TALK
ABOUT SEX, BABY

GLASGOW, 1992

It was New York hip hop trio Salt-N-Pepa who exhorted us to 'talk about sex' back in 1991, and although it was a sentiment met with a stony and embarrassed silence across many of the more stuffy breakfast tables of Britain, a chap by the name of Eddie Crawford thought further discussion was very much in order.

Specifically Eddie wanted to talk about runners and the sex of their children. Fortunately Eddie just happened to be a researcher at the University of Glasgow and was perfectly placed to investigate the effects of running on the gender of offspring. It is admittedly something of a niche subject but Eddie was undeterred and in 1992 published a paper entitled *Sex Ratio of the Children of Male Distance Runners*, which may have lacked a certain pizzazz in terms of its title, but did produce some startling conclusions.

Eddie's interest in the topic was not in truth piqued by the catchy chorus of Salt-N-Pepa's chart topper – it got to number one in Australia, Belgium, Germany, Holland and Switzerland – but by an article in *Scotland's Runner* which claimed just 23 per cent of children fathered by serious runners were male.

Being a science sort, Eddie knew that the average incidence of male births globally was 51 per cent and he was intrigued, as chaps in white coats and glasses often are, why runners appeared to father a disproportionate number of girls. He immediately dusted off his best biro and notebook and set to work.

A total of 139 male runners were approached to take part in the study. They were split into three groups – those taking a break from training, those running up to 30 miles (48.3km) per week and those diehards who were putting in between 30 and 50 miles (48.3–80.5km) every seven days. All Eddie had to do now was sit back and wait for some babies to arrive. Reports he attempted to speed up the process by procuring his subjects romantic weekend breaks in Paris are spurious to say the least.

In due course 377 bundles of joy arrived. The sex of each child was noted, and when Eddie analysed who was having girls and who was having boys, he came up with some intriguing results. The men who were not actively training at all had a 62 per cent chance of fathering a boy. The chaps however who ran up to 50 miles each week only had a 40 per cent of producing a son. It was all pretty conclusive stuff.

Now, concentrate, here comes the science bit. According to the study, high-volume running reduces the levels of testosterone in the male body, which in turn reduces the chances of producing boys. *Ipso facto* male marathon runners are more likely to have a home dominated by all things pink than their couch potato counterparts.

There's been little parallel research into the effect of running and women in terms of the gender of their children, but the theory is that high mileage will drive hormone levels and also increase the chances of having a daughter. If a couple are both training for a marathon at the same time, and aren't too knackered for some, ahem, 'together time', their chances of producing a girl theoretically go through the roof.

So forget expensive and intrusive in vitro fertilisation techniques, if you want to determine the gender of your next child, just be mindful of how often you lace up your trainers.

ULRICH GOES UNDER THE KNIFE

USA, 1992

Torture can manifest itself in many forms. For some there's no pain greater than the debilitating task of filling in a self-assessment tax return days before the HMRC deadline, or agonising whether to pass off the family visit to Uncle Bert as a business expense, while for others it's simply the prospect of watching one of the films of Mr Tom Cruise. Many would consider a day's paintballing in the Brecon Beacons, team building with Geoffrey from accounts and Barbara from HR, the ultimate torment.

Back in medieval times however they knew a thing or two about proper, old-fashioned torture, and if you were unfortunate enough to have displeased the local feudal grand fromage and hauled off to the nearest dungeon, you'd probably want to keep your shoes on lest the obligatory big fella in the black hood decided to pull your toenails off. Very slowly.

The painful practice of forcibly parting the nail from the toe was very *de rigueur* back then. It's been emulated as a no-frills form of torture by countless cultures ever since and if the bad guys can't lay their hands on some electrical cabling, an unprepossessing prison hidden in the desert or a few Alsatians, they'll go straight for the toes.

Strange, and potentially masochistic then, that acclaimed American ultramarathon runner Marshall Ulrich should voluntarily opt, albeit under the comforting embrace of a general anaesthetic, to have all ten of his own toenails permanently removed.

There is, however, method in Ulrich's apparent madness. 'A lot of runners have problems with their feet,' he explained. 'They get black toe, which is when you get a blister under the toenail and, in a few days, the toenail simply falls off. They were always in the process of falling off and growing back.'

OK, so that does makes sense but our American friend wasn't finished there, and in one of running's most disturbing ever examples of penny pinching, he decided his toes would not be the only part of his anatomy to go under the knife.

'I'd considered getting rid of the toenails before, but one night I was at a party with a surgeon friend,' he wrote in his book *Running On Empty*. 'I'd had a few and he said he'd do it cheap. He'd remove the toenails and perform a vasectomy at the same time, saving me some money by charging me for only one office visit. [My wife] Danielle was surprised – I hadn't told her what I was doing that day. Not too long before, she'd made an offhand remark about how I should get a vasectomy, so in my mind that meant we discussed it. The toes hurt a lot more than the testicles, for sure. I was back out running two days after the surgeries.'

One can only applaud Ulrich's dedication to his sport and sincerely hope the surgeon in question washed all his equipment thoroughly between the two rather contrasting procedures. Over the years other runners have had spinal discs removed, and even undergone breast reductions in pursuit of better times, but Ulrich's bizarre double remains the pinnacle of surgical silliness.

LITIGATION TO THE FORE!

LOUISIANA, USA, 1994

If you are of a squeamish disposition, you might want to skip past this particular tale, as it is eye-watering to say the very least. And don't say you haven't been warned because you have, and if you do insist on soldiering on through the paragraphs that follow, the responsibility is entirely your own.

It is 1994 and Robert McGuire was out for a jog with two friends in New Orleans. They decided to take a scenic route past the Bayou Oaks Golf Course, but after passing close by the third hole, an errant golf ball flew in their direction. The wayward sphere crashed onto the road next to the trio and bounced violently, deflecting into Robert's 'gentlemen's area'.

Now this would normally be no more than an amusing addition to an episode of *You've Been Framed* but the ball really smashed into poor Robert and ruptured his right testicle. You were warned, remember? The damage was severe and he had to have a part of his testicle surgically removed.

Of course this all occurred over in the good old US of A and there was an absolute flurry of litigation in the wake of the excruciating accident. Robert was sore in more ways than one and sued the New Orleans City Park Improvement Association, the body responsible for the golf course, claiming in legal papers that they had a duty to 'warn non-golfers on Palm Drive of the danger of golf balls and to configure the golf course so that a danger was not created for non-golfers on Palm Drive and to provide a protective barrier between the golf course and Palm Drive.'

City Park wasn't going to roll that easily and argued McGuire had 'jogged through the golf course between two clearly visible greens, which was not a hidden peril that required a warning or protective barrier. It was not reasonably foreseeable that a golfer would hit a ball so far to the right that a non-golfer would be injured.'

It was round one to City Park when the judge ruled in their favour but Robert's lawyer had a mortgage on a second house in Miami to pay for and urged him to appeal. A jury was brought in to sift the wheat from the chaff and they decided Robert did have a reasonable point and City Park was ordered to cough up $50,000 as settlement.

Cue yet another appeal and the whole unseemly business went all the way to the Supreme Court of Louisiana, which drew a final line under the painful matter when it decided City Park was not at fault. Robert didn't get a dime.

The moral of the story is twofold. The first is golf and jogging don't mix, and should you stumble across a course the next time you're out for a run, get the hell out of there as quickly as possible. The second, but equally important, is that American lawyers are never to be trusted and will have the shirt off your back if you're not careful.

RUN RABBIT, RUN
CALIFORNIA, USA, 1994

Rabbits are noted for their speed. It's all that practice they get running away from voracious foxes and evading irate farmers, and although Aesop's fabled hare did rather let the side down when it was beaten by the tortoise, the general rabbit vibe remains a rapid one.

Rabbits in the running world are equally quick. They do not boast fluffy white tails and prodigious front teeth because we're talking about pacemakers here, the athletes charged with ensuring a race is conducted at a reassuringly brisk pace, but we're stuck with the rabbit analogy now and, goddammit, we're going to see it through to the end.

So, in athletic parlance, a rabbit is a pace setter. They're usually bunged a few quid to come flying out of the blocks and take the rest of the field to the halfway point of a race in a decent time, before moving subserviently aside, simultaneously tugging their forelocks, to allow more illustrious athletes to romp home and maybe set a new world record. It's not exactly a glamorous job but somebody's got to do it, right?

The designated rabbit at the 1994 Los Angeles Marathon was a chap called Paul Pilkington. Paul was something of a specialist rabbit and the race organisers had coughed up $3,000 for his services that year, instructing him to take the field to the 15½ mile (24.9km) mark as quickly as he could.

The first 7 miles (11.3km) went according to plan as

Paul strode purposefully forward but it was at this stage a mischievous thought began to germinate in his mind. At the halfway stage, and still out in front all alone, his cheeky idea took root and by the time he hit 15½ miles and was supposed to defer to the chasing pack, it had become a fully formed decision. He was going to try and win the race.

'You have a minute and a half lead and you feel good, you should stop?' he said in an interview after the race. 'That's a pretty easy decision to make. I thought, nobody's going to catch me.' He was right and as he crossed the finishing line in a time of two hours, 12 minutes and 13 seconds, the rabbit was the champion.

Our story might end there, an amusing anecdote of a moment when the underdog triumphed, but while the spectators absolutely loved Paul's shock victory, some of the runners were less than impressed with what had just transpired.

Italy's Luca Barzaghi, the pre-race favourite, was absolutely spitting feathers. He had finished in second, 39 seconds adrift of Pilkington, but was bemused when he crossed the line and was presented with a mere silver medal, mistakenly believing he was victor. His face was a picture when he was quietly informed Paul had already picked up the winner's cheque. 'I thought the rabbit had dropped out,' ranted the angry Italian. 'Nobody told me he was still running. I thought I won. I was keeping my own pace. I was not running against him.' Barzaghi's interpreter then waded into the row. 'The rabbit is supposed to drop out of the race,' he fumed. 'Luca had no idea what was going on. It's not fair and we're going to do something about it.'

Get her. The Pilkington camp though wasn't going to take that from the Italians and his agent Bob Wood duly launched his own verbal broadside. 'Hey man, get a brain,' he screamed. 'You've got to be smart enough to know you aren't in first place. I know they give split times at this race. What, these guys can't read either? Those comments are bush league.'

It was all getting out of hand but the upshot was Paul hadn't actually broken any race rule and he, as far as the organisers were concerned, was the winner. His unexpected place in marathon history was assured while Barzaghi departed muttering darkly something about a horse's head.

THE MISGUIDED MEXICAN
NEW YORK, USA, 1994

It is a measure of the challenge that running a marathon represents that only the fittest and most dedicated dare attempt it. Those 26 miles and 385 yards can be a killer, and for all those who have successfully negotiated the distance, the sense of satisfaction is almost as big as their blisters.

Imagine then the madness of adding a little extra length to the race. Not on purpose, you understand, but inadvertently. Perhaps by taking a bit of an accidental detour before realising your mistake and legging it back to the approved route. Just an impromptu deviation, if you will.

Guess what? That's exactly what happened to Mexican runner Germán Silva at the New York Marathon in 1994, and although his little navigational miscalculation certainly wasn't in the plan, it did ultimately produce one of the most iconic, if bizarre, finishes in the event's history.

The race was in its last, pivotal mile. Silva was stride for stride with compatriot Benjamín Paredes, the rest of the field a distant memory, and as the two prepared for one final push to the finishing line, it was too close to call. The final stages of the course would take them through Central Park, but it was here that Silva dropped his dramatic clanger when he wrongly decided to follow the lead race car carrying members of the media down Seventh Avenue, while Paredes stuck to the correct route and headed down Columbus Circle.

It didn't take him long to realise the error of his way (both literally and metaphorically) but by the time he had retraced his steps and returned to the correct course, Paredes was 40 yards (27.4m) in front, and it seemed as though Silva was doomed to join the ranks of Devon Loch, Jean van de Velde and Jana Novotna, and snatch defeat from the jaws of victory.

It was time for an effort of superhuman proportions. The kick duly came as Silva ran the final mile of the race (plus those extra, accidental yards) in just five minutes and 15 seconds and he powered his way to an incredible victory, a mere two seconds in front of Paredes.

'I guess I got distracted by focusing so much on my winning strategy,' Silva told the *Runner's World* website. 'I was already thinking about the last half mile [0.8km]. So I followed the press motor. Then a police officer shouted and waved. While chasing Paredes, the only thing I hoped for was that the distance would be long enough to catch him, at least more than 600m [656 yards]. We regularly trained together, so I knew I had the best kick, and was fast enough to catch him if I had time.'

His misadventure but eventual triumph earned him the affectionate nickname 'Wrong Way Silva' from the aforementioned press, who were certainly enamoured of the Mexican after he had furnished them with the golden opportunity to run the headline 'Silva Lining'. He was inducted into the New York Road Runners Hall of Fame in 2014 to celebrate the twentieth anniversary of his success. Unfortunately the ceremony had to be briefly delayed when Silva got lost *en route* to the event.

MILES OF MONOTONY
NEW YORK, USA, 1997

One of the greatest pleasures of running are the views. Whether you're an urban or rural jogger, there are such vistas out there to feast your eyes upon and if you plan your route with even a vestige of imagination or a cursory glance at Google Maps, no two runs need ever be the same.

Unless that is you happen to enter the annual Self-Transcendence 3100 Mile Race in New York, which, even with the best will in the world, is as mind-numbingly boring as it is gruelling, and if you embark on the event hoping to see all the nooks and crannies of the Big Apple, you're going to be sorely disappointed indeed.

The brainchild of a spiritualist chap called Sri Chinmoy, the urban ultramarathon was first run in 1997, and according to the event website was founded because our Sri believed 'peace could be manifested through silent meditation, music, poetry, art and sports.'

It's undeniably an arduous race with runners beginning their exertions at six every morning. They must average 59 miles (95.9km) per day for 52 straight days to clock up the magic 3,100 mile (4,988km) milestone. That equates to an average of 18 hours on the road each day and unsurprisingly only 37 competitors had finished the event between 1997 and 2014.

'The Supreme doesn't want you to be satisfied with 50m,' Sri once said. 'He wants you to run 51m, 52m, 54m ....

Otherwise, if you always aim at the same goal, it becomes monotonous.'

And herein lies the problem because the Self-Transcendence 3100 Mile Race has to be the most monotonous event ever conceived in the history of running. Seriously, it's so tedious entrants are in as much danger of suffering death by boredom, as they are blisters or shin splints.

The course is a circle around the Thomas A. Edison Vocational Technical High School in Queens and 100 times per day the runners lap the modest college campus and surrounding streets. They never veer off and the sense of *déjà vu* must be utterly overwhelming. To add insult to injury, it's not a particularly pretty route either.

'Five lean, sun-baked runners with bulging calf muscles make their way around and around and around a dirty red brick high school building,' reported *The Washington Post* during the event in 1998. 'From before dawn until well after dark, they have jogged this same, wearying route over asphalt sidewalks, alongside the iron gate that surrounds the school, down a noisy roadway that spits car exhaust and past a dusty baseball diamond. They have run past kids in baggy jeans, idling cars with rap music blaring and an abandoned black Mazda with no tires, busted windows and everything – from seats to the gas cap – stripped.'

It does rather beg the question why Sri, who shuffled off this mortal coil in 2007, decided to stage his strange race around a school in Queens when all the sights and sounds of New York City were right on his doorstep.

Sri once dabbled with the idea of staging an ultramarathon in the UK around the roundabouts of Milton Keynes but abandoned the project on the basis the course would be far too stimulating for the competitors.

OBSTACLE COURSE WITH A STING

WOLVERHAMPTON, 1998

For many the highlight of the annual school sports day is the obstacle course. After all, it's so much more interesting than a straight, predictable sprint, more physically challenging than the egg and spoon race and infinitely more graceful than the awkward spectacle that is the bizarre wheelbarrow race.

It's amazing what ingenious PE teachers can achieve with a few adroitly positioned cones, a liberal sprinkling of bean bags and, of course, a strategically placed pommel horse. *Voila!* A fiendish obstacle course to test the mettle of the finest athletes Year Six has to offer. Or any parents determined to get themselves on *You've Been Framed*.

Such childish courses however pale into insignificance when compared to the challenges faced by those idiotic enough to enter the annual Nettle Warrior event, a race staged on an 8 mile (12.9km) course on a farm outside Wolverhampton, which puts the 'O' (my god!) into obstacle courses.

Ominously billed as 'the most dangerous test of mental and physical pain, fear and endurance' (or maybe that was the *Relate* guide to a successful marriage?), the Nettle Warrior was first staged in 1998, and requires runners to complete two circuits of what is affectionately called 'The Killing Fields'. *En route* they must negotiate a myriad of obstacles miscellaneously dubbed Colditz Walls, the Behemoth, the

Dead Leg Swamp, Stalag Escape and the Death Plunge, plus countless other mud traps, hills, cargo netting and rope crossings. The introduction of the obstacle 'The Nice Cup of Tea and a Sit Down' proved a disastrous innovation and was abandoned after just one year.

The Nettle Warrior is the brainchild of one Billy Wilson, a former battalion barber in the Grenadier Guards, and he is very much from the old school when it comes to athletic pursuits.

'I wanted to teach people how to be tough,' he said. 'It's not a race, it's an event. It's for people to come and challenge the Tough Guy course. Everybody here is a winner. I saw people sitting on buses in the early Seventies, day after day, looking miserable, and I thought, I need to get those people off those buses and out in the fresh air. So I set up jogging exercises in the park and encouraged people to jump fences, which was unheard of in those days. Those small fences grew into vast obstacles, and Tough Guy was born.'

Getting fit and active is undeniably admirable, but exactly why Billy decided his assault course would also require competitors to run through waist-high nettles (the clue's in the name), as well as risk electric shocks from overhanging wire cables is intriguing. The word masochist does rather readily spring to mind.

The race is held every July, which means runners also have to contend with the dangers of sunburn on top of sheer exhaustion, nettle stings and involuntarily electrocution. Billy did suggest adding a rogue sniper element to the race but confidants persuaded him it was probably a step too far.

HOT PANTS IN HAWAII

HAWAII, USA, 1998

The purpose of satire is to hold a mirror up to society, forcing it whether it likes it or not to confront unpalatable truths and mend, in theory at least, the error of its abhorrent ways. There are those who are not convinced *Have I Got News For You* has really had that much of an impact on modern Britain but *Private Eye* does run some jolly funny cartoons and fixing the nation is a job for those snake oil salesmen and women in Government, isn't it?

But back to running, while seamlessly maintaining the satire theme, and one of the most unusual and risqué races around, the annual Kona Underpants Run in Hawaii. It does exactly what it says on the tin and each year the assembled entrants tackle a gentle 1½ mile (2.4km) course in only their undies. Admittedly the ladies are quite reasonably permitted something to cover their chests, and everyone's allowed to pop on a pair of trainers, but it's very much all about the underwear.

The event is not, as you may have initially suspected, an elaborate excuse for some inappropriate leering. For a start, it raises a lot of money for local charidees, but the real reason it was founded by three triathlete friends back in 1998 is more satirical than you might have imagined.

For those not familiar with the triathlon community, Kona is also the scene of the Ironman World Championship and each year ahead of the event a throng of unfeasibly buff athletes descend on the area. The problem was they weren't exactly overdoing it in the sartorial stakes.

'We had been racing in Kona since the mid-1980s and after a couple of years, it dawned on us that a lot of the athletes would stroll around town in their Speedos,' Paul Huddle, one of the Underpants Run's original founders, told the *Triathlon Competitor* website. 'We just thought it was funny but we also started to witness first hand how it offended the locals.

'The wearing of Speedos became epidemic and, frankly it was a problem. Here we were, guests in this great little community, and we were offending the sensibilities of the locals in their day-to-day lives. As a way of showing everyone how silly it looks and, therefore, hoping to decrease the number of offenders, we decided to do a little protest jog. There were just three of us so it was mildly unnerving to start with but we got a lot of laughs and realized that most people "got it". The next year we had 30 and it's grown each year since then.'

Gotcha. Parodying the heinous budgie smugglers while raising some cash for the local orphanage. Clever boys. What the locals make of their brazen attempt to preserve decorum and defend decency, which does after all encourage the flaunting of even more flesh, is a different story.

THE WONDER OF WIM

FINLAND, 1999

It's an argument among runners, which generates a ferocity only witnessed between frustrated bargain hunters when IKEA has a sale on, and they run out of those cheap Billy bookcases. Or when Members of Parliament debate whether dinner with the in-laws at Claridges, wine, coffee and *dégustifs* included, is a legitimate expenses claim.

Our big running row centres on the thorny topic of temperature, and whether it is better to step out in the warm embrace of a hot summer's day, or take to the streets on a frosty January morning. The 'hot or cold?' debate has been raging for years among joggers and has been known to ruin friendships, wreck marriages and even cause wars. That last one might not be true.

The two camps remain diametrically opposed with the 'hotters' insisting a warm backdrop to a run loosens muscles, reduces the risk of injury and boosts your tan. The 'colders' maintain a chilly jog precludes lots of unseemly sweating and dehydration, and keeps you moving in a bid not to freeze.

It is safe to assume Dutch lunatic Wim Hof is an advocate of a bracing run. In fact as far as Wim is concerned, the colder the better, and the list of his freezing feats is as long as it is bizarre.

It all began for Wim in 1999, when he headed inside the Arctic Circle and the north of Finland, to attempt a half marathon. It was no ordinary race though because Wim tackled the course in just a pair of shorts. No trainers. No running vest of any description. It was -4°F (-20°C) but Wim still made it home.

In 2007 he set a world record for the fastest half marathon barefoot on ice after another foray to Finland, finishing in two hours, 16 minutes and 34 seconds, while in 2009 he went the full distance by completing 26 miles 385 yards inside the Arctic Circle. Admittedly he did wear a pair of flimsy sandals for that particular challenge, but he remained bare-chested, and it was still extremely bloody cold. In those conditions, and without protective clothing, a normal person would lose consciousness after an hour.

The secret of Wim's ability to, well, not freeze to death is that he can control his own internal body thermostat, and when things gets a bit chilly, he can raise his core body temperature with the power of his mind. And even the Jedi can't do that.

'I had a stroll like this in the park with somebody and I saw the ice and I thought, what would happen if I go in there,' Wim said by way of explanation of how he had discovered his unique skill. 'I was really attracted to it. I went in, got rid of my clothes. Thirty seconds I was in and a tremendous good feeling when I came out and since then, I repeated it every day.'

'For me, God is cold. I think of the cold as a noble force. It's just helping me, training me. It's bringing me back to nature the way it was meant to be. And this way, I not only endure the cold, I love the cold. I know my body, I know my mind, I know what I can do.'

Wim's amazing exploits obviously gave the 'colders' cause for celebration, championing as he did the virtues of refrigerated running, but he did rather betray the cause when he successfully completed a marathon in the Namib Desert without water. Which left the 'colders' very hot under the collar indeed.

PAULA'S KNEE
NIGHTMARES

UK, 2000

Now if you think for one moment the inestimable Paula Radcliffe is going to make an appearance in this book on the basis of one unfortunate lavatorial mishap during the London Marathon in 2005 you've got another think coming. Radcliffe's years of long and loyal service to British running should surely eclipse any memories of her impromptu 'comfort break' and let's all agree to never mention the whole beastly business again.

No, Paula's inclusion on this page comes courtesy of her unfortunate propensity to pick up extremely bizarre knee injuries, which mere mortals could only dream of sustaining.

The first came in 2001 after her wedding to Gary Lough. It was, by all accounts, a splendid occasion, and not long after the big day, Paula determined she was going to sit down and write thank you letters for all the lovely presents. Not to Cousin Anne and Albert for the 'his and hers' nasal hair trimmers, but that's a different story.

The problem was that Paula didn't sit down. She kneeled. For far too long. And when she finally stood up something clicked, and rather than heading to the Post Office it was a trip to hospital, minor surgery and 13 weeks on the sidelines. She could of course have simply emailed all her guests to express her gratitude but Paula's a bit of a traditionalist in that way.

She sustained her second strange knee injury in the build-up to the Olympic Games in Athens in 2004. Out for a training run, a car speeded past her and propelled a loose stone at high speed in her direction, the sharp projectile slamming into her knee and leaving Paula in an unceremonious heap. It was no laughing matter. The injury meant she lost two-and-a-half weeks of crucial training and she was only able to run again a few days before the race. Unsurprisingly she was not 100 per cent at the Olympic Marathon and after 22 agonising miles (25.4km) battling the pain, Paula was forced to accept the inevitable and pull up.

'The British press, unaware of her problems, branded her a choker,' wrote Sean Ingle in *The Guardian*. 'Some of that reputation has stuck – unfairly – because Radcliffe never revealed the extent of her problems.'

Paula's career – three London Marathon and three New York Marathon triumphs and the women's world record – wasn't half bad of course despite her misfortunes, but what more she might have achieved if she hadn't been blighted by bizarre injuries is tantalising.

She hung up her spikes after competing at the London Marathon in 2015 but her legacy, if sadly not her knees, remains very much intact. 'She gave women permission to feel they could go out and run and be part of the London Marathon,' said Sebastian Coe. 'A generation of runners, male and female, have taken up the sport because of Paula Radcliffe.'

LLOYD'S LOCH ADVENTURE

SCOTTISH HIGHLANDS, 2003

Do you remember the 2002 London Marathon? It was the year in which an American chap called Khalid Khannouchi set a new world record with a time of two hours, five minutes and 38 seconds, while Paula Radcliffe set a new course record as she swept aside all challengers in the women's field.

Both were impressive feats we can all agree, but the coverage of the race was rather hijacked by a comedian by the name of Lloyd Scott, who completed the course wearing an antique deep sea diving suit. You know, one of those unwieldy, old-fashioned outfits with the metal helmet and the big, heavy boots.

It took Lloyd five days and eight hours to finally finish his marathon and, as Andy Warhol so presciently predicted, his 15 minutes of fame duly arrived as the press lapped up his uplifting story of determination and courage. Or idiocy and brazen attention seeking, depending entirely on your point of view.

But that fleeting taste of fame wasn't enough for Lloyd. Oh no, he wanted more, much more, and the following year he decided to attempt the world's first ever underwater marathon. In Loch Ness no less. In his diving suit.

Now if that didn't get him a few column inches, nothing would, and Lloyd intrepidly set off in September from Fort Augustus at the southern end of the loch. Thirteen days later he emerged at Lochend, near Inverness, and by virtue of being the first man to attempt the distance, he was the new underwater marathon world record holder.

It hadn't been all plain sailing beneath the surface. A 15ft (4.6m) tumble early on during the 'race' had left him with a badly bruised shoulder and there were also problems with his oxygen supply.

'I've had to cope with poor visibility, which has at times been nil,' he said after emerging from the water. 'I've had to work against the resistance and the pressure of the water. You don't know what's underfoot. Sometimes it's mud, silt, rocks or nothing.'

'The airline also kept getting caught and I also had to deal with a build-up of carbon dioxide in the helmet. It's also very cold and very lonely. It's definitely been far more difficult doing it underwater than it has been on land.'

It's the water that makes it tougher, Lloyd, all the water.

The burning question of course, is whether he caught any glimpses of a giant, possibly prehistoric, beast lurking in the depths during his fortnight-long foray. The Loch Ness Tourist Board was keeping all its fingers crossed, but sadly no, Lloyd admitted the extent of his sightings of aquatic life was 'two fish'. Definitely not what the Loch Ness Tourist Board was hoping for.

Since his Scottish adventure, Lloyd has among many other feats cycled from Perth to Sydney on a penny farthing, completed the Great North Run in a spaceman's suit and entered the London Marathon again, this time wearing a full suit of armour. His exploits have raised plenty of money for good causes but sadly for Lloyd not yet secured him a coveted place on *The One Show* sofa.

MONKEY BUSINESS
LONDON, 2003

If you're familiar with the acclaimed *Planet of the Apes* film franchise, you'll be accustomed to the sight of hordes of monkeys running down city streets. By the way, did you know that the collective noun for monkeys is a barrel? And, apparently, also a cartload. And tribe. Or troop. And wilderness. Anyway if you're not acquainted with Cornelius, Dr Zaius *et al*, and happen to be wandering around central London in September, you're in for one hell of a simian surprise.

That is because each year the streets of the capital play host to the annual 'Great Gorilla Run' and, to be fair, if no one has warned you that hundreds of apes are going to be charging across Tower Bridge and Embankment, it's going to come as something of a considerable shock. Even when you realise it's only a bunch of animal-loving fun runners in fancy dress.

First staged in 2003, the 'Great Gorilla Run' is held over an 8km (5 mile) course and has attracted thousands of entrants over the years, raising money for mountain gorilla charities in central Africa. And don't worry if you haven't got your own monkey suit, the organisers helpfully provide one to all entrants once your cheque has cleared.

The race is, of course, a gift to newspapers and journalists with a penchant for puns. 'Some might say they are bananas,' reported *The Daily Mail* in 2010, 'but almost

600 people dressed in gorilla suits were running wild in London yesterday.' Celebrities have flocked to support the event but they evidently all got lost *en route* in 2014 and only Uri Geller turned up. 'Your mind power is giving the gorillas the energy to survive,' everyone's least favourite spoon bender announced, 'and my mind power gave you the energy to get through 8km.' So not all the training and preparation then, Uri.

The run's website is bursting with information about the event, and handy tips for entrants, and none more so than their suggested Spotify list of tracks runners might like to listen to during the race. 'Apeman' by the Kinks? Obviously. 'Jungle Boogie' by Kool & the Gang? If you absolutely insist. But did you know there's actually a track called 'Go-Go Gorilla'? By a band called The Surfin' Gorillas. Genius.

All the relevant authorities are forewarned about the 'Great Gorilla Run' to avoid panic on the streets of London and it's a prudent precaution because there are dangers in dressing up as an ape and charging about the place. Take, for example, the poor bugger who donned a gorilla suit in 2014 and proceeded to race around the Loro Parque zoo on Tenerife as part of an emergency drill to assess how the zoo would react if a real ape escaped. It was all going swimmingly until a short-sighted vet mistook the zoo employee for an actual AWOL simian and promptly shot him with a tranquiliser dart loaded with enough sedative to bring down a 400lb (181kg) gorilla. According to the Spanish media the bloke in the suit went, ahem, bananas when he finally came round.

THE BRAZEN SEX DOCTOR

GERMANY, 2004

The sex therapy business is booming. Long gone are the days when those having problems in the bedroom would reach for a copy of the *Kama Sutra* or don a pair of sunglasses and take a furtive trip to Ann Summers. No, these days if things aren't particularly pyrotechnic in between the sheets, the first port of call for those desperate to attain amorous enlightenment is a therapist.

How exactly one qualifies as a love doctor is a grey area. Do you have to be good at 'it' yourself to qualify for the certificate? How much 'practical' research is required? What the hell happens in the final exam? These are all intriguing questions but, sadly, not strictly relevant to our current story.

The German sex therapist, Dr Peter Niehenke, is however absolutely apposite to this tale. Central, in fact, and although he is considered by many of his patients to be a guru on all matters carnal, it is his running exploits that have made him something of a celebrity in Germany.

The good doctor loves a jog. He's always out on the roads around his home in Freiburg, clocking up the miles and working on his stamina. The problem is Niehenke refuses to wear a stitch of clothing on his jaunts and it's landed him in rather a lot of trouble with the German Old Bill over the years.

His conviction for indecent exposure in 2004 after stepping

out starkers in a local Freiburg park, resulting in a €600 fine, was merely the latest in a long list of naked indiscretions and every time he's collared by the boys in blue, it's not long before the doctor is pulling on his trainers and pulling off his clothes once again. By 2004 he had amassed almost *de rigueur* 2,500 in fines and made numerous appearances in court.

Niehenke always argues that jogging in the buff is 'sexually liberating' (although he would say that, wouldn't he?) and insists there is no specific law that forbids a spot of nudey perambulation. The judge in 2004, however, wasn't having that and ruled that the 'court does not support the defendant's view that running naked in public is one of his civil rights.' Niehenke fought the law and the law won.

A slightly distasteful footnote to the doctor's story is the exact nature of this exposure. Many of the reports concerning the court case maintained Niehenke took to the streets in no more than his socks and trainers but one despatch had it that he actually ran with a nylon stocking over his genitals 'to keep them warm'.

It's difficult to decide which would be the more disturbing sight – a fully naked sex therapist speeding past or one with a pair of tights strategically attached to his groin. May you be spared from ever having to make such a distasteful choice.

THE GREAT ESCAPE
LOUISIANA, USA, 2006

As every canny criminal knows, running can be jolly helpful when it comes to avoiding the long arm of the law. Nowadays the police might be aided and abetted by thermal imaging cameras, helicopters, sniffer dogs and unfeasibly loud sirens, in their pursuit of the criminal fraternity, but there are times when simply legging it is good enough to evade capture. Especially if the officer in pursuit has been overdoing it on the doughnuts.

Our tale here, however, is evidence that sometimes you don't even need to break into a sweat to stay one step ahead of the combined might of law enforcement.

The ne'er-do-well that interests us here is Richard Lee McNair, a naughty American who was banged up for murder in the 1980s, but proved rather adept at escaping from prison. His third and final bid for freedom in 2006 saw him break out of the United States Penitentiary in Pollock, Louisiana, after he hid in a specially constructed 'escape pod', which was shrink-wrapped, hidden under some mail bags and fork-lifted to a nearby warehouse.

A few hours after his successful breakout, McNair found himself by the side of a rural road when one of Louisiana's boys in blue pulled up in his patrol car, and started asking him questions. The radio waves were alight with talk of an escaped prisoner and the officer suspected he'd got his man.

McNair had to think quickly. Fortunately for him he was wearing trainers, shorts and a tight, *Die Hard*-style vest and when quizzed about what he was doing, he said he was out for a jog. A ten-minute exchange between McNair and the officer ensued in which the escapee gave two different aliases but he stuck to his running story.

We know details of the conversation because the whole thing was recorded by the dash cam in the officer's car. McNair explained away his lack of ID on the grounds you don't carry your wallet while out for a jog, and despite radioing HQ for a description of the prisoner, the officer bought it and McNair was allowed to continue with his 'run'.

He was on the loose for 18 months but in late 2007 he made the mistake of trying to evade the Royal Canadian Mounted Police, who as we all know, always get their man. This time McNair did attempt to leg it when he was spotted driving a van in New Brunswick but after abandoning his wheels, the pursuing Mounties proved too fleet of foot (or hoof) for him and he was arrested. 'During a brief pursuit, the van turned onto a dead-end backwoods road and the driver bolted on foot,' reported the local newspaper. 'McNair ran about 400m [437 yards] before being tackled by one of the officers.'

His claim that he was training for the Quebec Marathon fell on deaf ears and the American penal system has managed to keep McNair securely behind bars ever since.

THE SPACE RACE
INTERNATIONAL SPACE STATION, 2007

'Space, the final frontier,' Captain James T. Kirk used to intone before each and every episode of *Star Trek*. 'These are the voyages of the star ship *Enterprise*. Its five-year mission: to explore strange new worlds, to seek out new life and new civilizations, to boldly go where no man has gone before.'

What exactly the women were meant to be doing while Kirk and the chaps were messing about with their phasers was never stipulated, despite repeated requests from Uhura and the rest of the girls for clarification, but the point is that the early days of space travel, albeit entirely fictional, were rather sexist.

Those days, however, are long gone and in 2007 a lady by the name of Sunita 'Suni' Williams struck a blow for women in space and the girls in general when the American astronaut became the first ever person to attempt to run a marathon in orbit around the Earth.

Suni's struggle with the 26-and-a-bit miles took place on board the International Space Station in April and was timed to coincide exactly with the staging of the Boston Marathon, in which her fellow astronaut Karen Nyberg was running, a few hundred miles below her. The ISS's best treadmill was duly booked for the day (much to the chagrin of the Russian cosmonaut on board who really fancied doing a quick 10K) and once she'd been safely strapped down to counteract the effects of zero gravity, she was ready and at the same moment as the elite runners in Boston set off, her challenge began. The harness apparently proved a bit of a problem, as it chafed somewhat on Suni's shoulders and hips, but she refused to quit and 'crossed the line' in a respectable four hours and 24 minutes.

'The idea came up because I'm a big proponent of physical fitness and I just wanted to make kids aware that it is a necessary part of your life,' Suni explained. 'I think if I could do something up here to show kids that it's fun and it's important, then maybe somebody will get off the couch and start working out.'

Obviously you don't necessarily need to blast off from Cape Canaveral to follow Suni's example. A gentle jog on *terra firma* is perfectly acceptable.

Suni herself returned to Earth later in 2007 after a record 192-day stint in space, and in 2008 she ran the Boston Marathon for real, but she was back to her old tricks four years later when she became the first person to complete a triathlon in space. Once again Suni timed her attempt to coincide with a real event – the Nautica Malibu Triathlon in Southern California – and after swimming for ½ mile (0.8km), cycling for 18 miles (30km) and running for 4 miles (6.4km), she clocked a time of one hour, 48 minutes and 33 seconds.

A swimming pool in space? Wouldn't all the water float to the ceiling? Well, yes, so Suni used special weights to simulate the swimming element of the event.

Suni is nothing if not intrepid and her next celestial challenge is rumoured to be an ultramarathon in space, proving conclusively that once you've grown tired of floating around and eating cornflakes in mid-air, there really is bugger all to do on the ISS.

THE HARRIERS' FLOUR FAUX PAS

CONNECTICUT, USA, 2007

It was back in 2004 that the hunting of hares with more than two hounds was outlawed in Britain. It was, depending on whether you happened to own a sprawling country pile in Shropshire or a two-bed flat in Clapham, another example of political correctness gone mad or a victory for common sense, but the fact is that hares have it just that little bit easier in rural Blighty these days.

For certain runners over in the States though, hare and hounds means something quite different. It is neither a centuries old, traditional country pastime, nor a barbaric and archaic form of animal cruelty (your view again depending on the above criteria), but a fun way of enlivening a group jog and sees a couple of lead runners (the hares) mark out a trail for their colleagues (the hounds) to follow. There's absolutely no killing, or politics, involved.

One group that was particularly fond of hare and hound races was the Hash House Harriers from Connecticut, a club that rather charmingly described itself as a 'drinking club with a running problem'. The members just couldn't get enough of the format but in 2007 it landed them in a whole heap of unanticipated bother with the local authorities.

Our hares for the day were Dr Daniel Salchow and his sister Dorothee and they set off late in the afternoon to mark a 4 mile (6.4km) trail for the rest of the club. Around 40 minutes later the job was done and Daniel and Dorothee retired to the good doctor's house to wait for the hounds to join them for a well-deserved drinkie.

It was then his wife phoned to tell him there was a bit of a problem. A massive problem actually and he'd better get his arse down to the car park of the local Ikea – through which the pair had routed the hounds – pronto. He was confronted by the disconcerting scene of scores of policemen and chaps in chemical suits cordoning off the area and everyone looking jolly worried.

Daniel and Dorothee had used flour to mark out their course, but we live in an era of heightened anxieties and when someone saw the pair liberally sprinkling white powder all over the car park, they jumped to the conclusion it was anthrax. Cue a major bioterrorism alert and the deployment of lots of chaps with specialist equipment. The scare forced Ikea to be shut down and scores of customers returned home without their Billy bookcases.

When Daniel turned up he forlornly tried to explain the situation to Connecticut's finest. He offered to taste the powder to prove it was innocuous, he even offered to sweep the mess up, but the Old Bill were deaf to his pleas and promptly slapped the cuffs on.

It soon emerged that the powder was indeed merely flour but the police department were not happy. The silence of their tills made Ikea very grumpy and the local Mayor was in a foul mood too. 'You see powder,' said a spokeswoman for the city, 'and you never know.' Daniel was charged with a first-degree breach of the peace, a felony, while the Old Bill, Ikea and the Mayor all considered suing the doctor for damages.

In the end common sense prevailed, and it was agreed that Daniel and the Hash House Harriers would work with the city and Ikea on a fundraiser to benefit local charities, as a way of making amends for the kerfuffle he had caused. 'It was absolutely not in any way what we intended,' he said, breathing a sigh of relief, 'and not what we anticipated.'

THE PRESTON PACE MAN

LANCASHIRE, 2007

It was Mahatma Gandhi who once said, 'There is more to life than increasing its speed.' Mahatma was of course not an athlete – he was too busy ending colonial rule in India and extolling the virtues of nonviolent civil disobedience – but had he ever discarded his trademark sandals and popped on a pair of spikes, he'd soon have realised that going faster is of course the *raison d'être* of the runner.

A more apt quote for the running fraternity can be found in the film *Top Gun* when Maverick declares, 'I feel the need, the need for speed.' It's not often we'd give Tom Cruise top billing over Gandhi, but we live in strange times, and for once the diminutive Hollywood heart-throb had a point.

The fastest on the planet on two feet is of course Usain Bolt. The two-time Olympic champion is jolly quick indeed, and in a 100m race in Berlin back in 2009, the Jamaican was clocked at one stage sprinting at a world record 27¾mph (44.7km/h). He averaged 23⅓mph (37.6km/h) over the full distance and crossed the line after a mere 9.58 seconds on the track, which still stands as the world record for the event. Yep, Usain was seriously rapid in Germany that day.

His efforts however pale into insignificance compared to the Lancashire runner who, two years earlier, was clocked doing a pretty impressive 230mph (370km/h) through the streets of Preston. And there's a photograph on the World Wide Web to prove it.

Sadly the reason for our unnamed athlete's incredible velocity was not a revolutionary new training regime, a favourable tailwind or even a burning desire to become the first British Olympic 100m champion since Linford Christie, but in fact a faulty speed indicator sign that had been recently erected but had a few wires loose.

The good folk of Preston had begun to suspect their new sign was faulty when passing cars were told they were travelling through the town at 100mph (161km/h) when they knew full well, officer, that they still hadn't got out of third gear, but before the Lancashire Partnership for Road Safety were able to send over some chaps with screwdrivers to fix the problem, the cheeky runner had taken the opportunity to scamper past the machine and get a picture of himself doing an unprecedented 230mph. Well you would, wouldn't you?

'When it was first installed I thought it was a good idea because it reminds drivers of their speed and tells them to slow down,' said one local. 'But when you are driving along doing 30mph and it's telling you you're going much faster, it's ridiculous. Even Lewis Hamilton would have difficulty getting up to those speeds.' Or indeed even Mr Bolt.

Our opportunistic jogger wrote to *Guinness World Records* asking to be recognised as the fastest man on the planet but was informed they weren't born yesterday and told as politely as possible never to contact them again.

RUN MARRED BY MARS
TYNE AND WEAR, 2008

As we have already touched upon, there are many perils associated with what should be a danger-free jog. If runners were a paranoid bunch they could be forgiven for feeling rather victimised, such is the myriad of potential dangers out there, and the number of injuries that often ensue.

There are essentially two basic groups of potential pitfalls: the first is the mundane and predictable, and what jogger hasn't eyed up a pothole, an irate Yorkshire Terrier or a small child on a scooter with suspicion, and whenever possible given them a wide, wide berth.

Then of course there are the dangers you could never have imagined – the obstacles that both literally and metaphorically you never saw coming. We're talking here about the bizarre perils that even the most gnarled of runners would never have predicted in a million years.

'A jogger was injured after being hit by a frozen Mars Bar hurled from a passing car,' reported the *Hartlepool Mail* website in 2008. 'The man was running along Sunderland Road, South Shields, when the rock-hard chocolate bar was thrown at him. Police said the car – a black Nissan or Toyota – then turned round, drove back past the shocked man, and its occupants threw another object at him before driving off. The bizarre incident, which resulted in the man suffering a swollen ankle, happened at about 10.30a.m. yesterday.'

Crocked by chilled confectionery? That's an injury they

definitely don't list in *Jogging for Beginners*.

The incident does beg some interesting but disturbing questions. Did our drive-by assailants deliberately arm themselves with frozen chocolate or did they just happen to have the Mars Bar in the glove compartment? Was it a random attack or did they know the identity of our fallen runner? Why didn't they throw a Snickers? Or a KitKat Chunky Mint? Intriguingly the incident took place in January, so perhaps the Mars Bar was frozen *al fresco* before it was launched at the jogger.

Sadly the police never made any significant progress in the hunt for the elusive chocolate chuckers. The Mars Bar didn't yield any fingerprints, primarily because it was wolfed down by the investigating officers at their next tea break, and there were no eyewitnesses to the incident other than the victim. The area wasn't covered by CCTV and, unsurprisingly, the culprits themselves never came forward.

The Mars Bar attack of 2008 may not be a mystery to rival the disappearance of Lord Lucan or the popularity of *The X Factor*, but it does serve as reminder to all joggers that danger lurks around every corner, and sometimes that danger can even be covered in delicious milk chocolate.

EKVALL'S GOTHENBURG HORROR

SWEDEN, 2008

In many ways the Internet is a truly wonderful invention, which has enriched millions of people's lives, deepened the well of human knowledge and made it fantastically easy to order a cut-price pair of Levi's 501s from Vietnam at 3 o'clock in the morning. The unsolicited adverts for Viagra and the countless videos of kittens doing the funniest things are admittedly an irritation but, all in all, the World Wide Web is still generally viewed as a good thing.

The views of Swedish runner Mikael Ekvall on the Internet are not documented but it's probably safe to assume he's not a big fan, since it is a medium that is responsible for what should have been 15 minutes of infamy becoming a lifetime of shame. Like an elephant or the taxman, the World Wide Web never forgets.

Mikael's story revolves around the Gothenburg Half Marathon of 2008. He was only a teenager at the time and had to really dig deep to finish the race but unfortunately he rather over-exerted himself and, how to put this delicately, soiled himself mid-race. To add insult to injury, a photographer was on hand to capture the image of a grimacing Ekvall with a brown discharge seeping through his shorts and dripping down his legs.

In a different era, Mikael's misfortune would perhaps have merited a picture in the local rag the next day and the whole sorry incident would have been quickly forgotten but the World Wide Web has ensured the unpleasant image of his moment of misery lives in perpetuity. Type 'Mikael Ekvall' into any search engine and scatological proof will be immediately forthcoming. Don't say you were not warned.

Mikael was asked by reporters in the immediate aftermath of the race why he hadn't made a brief detour, grabbed a wet wipe and freshened up. 'No, I'd lose time,' he replied. 'If you quit once, it's easy to do it again and again and again. It becomes a habit.' The whole sorry business earned Ekvall the nickname 'Bajsmannen', which roughly translates as 'poop man'.

For the record, Mikael finished the half marathon in 2008 in a respectable twenty-first place, despite his mishap, and was back in Gothenburg the following year and came home in ninth. He has subsequently represented Sweden at the European Athletics Championships and in 2014 he set a national record for the half marathon after racing in Copenhagen. Thanks to the Internet and its seemingly infinite storage capacity however, Bajsmannen's athletic exploits are still largely eclipsed by his momentary loss of control back in 2008, and the images that stubbornly linger online.

RUNNING ON RUBBER
LONDON, 2008

For most marathon runners, a good pair of trainers is prerequisite kit before embarking on their arduous 26 miles and 385 yards. It's a hell of a long way to attempt to run if your feet ain't nice and comfy, and even if you're not going to see any change out of £100 or more after your visit to Sports Direct, it's probably money well spent as the big race beckons.

That means the estimated 35,000 runners who entered the London Marathon in 2008 collectively spent somewhere north of £3.5million on footwear and that is, we can all surely agree, a hell of a lot of cash. For six of the field, however, no money changed hands in exchange for their all-important race footwear.

Our thrifty group were all Maasai warriors from northern Tanzania, and while their fellow marathoners were all pounding the streets of the Big Smoke in Adidas, Asics or Nike, the Africans remarkably tackled the course shod in running shoes made from recycled car tyres, held together with iron nails. The poor sods didn't have a gel-cushioned sole between them.

Made by local craftsmen, the 'trainers' cost our Tanzanian athletes one goat for a pair (and that's absolutely true) and according to *Daily Mail* reporter Rob Draper, who gave the unusual footwear a try, they were every bit as uncomfortable for the uninitiated as they sound.

'I could manage barely half a mile when I tried out their improvised footwear after the Maasai kindly lent me a pair to road-test over a section of the marathon course along London's Embankment,' he wrote. 'Perhaps it is the distinctive regimental running style of the Maasai, which looks more like bouncing along rather than striding, that renders the home-made trainers so effective for the warriors. But try to run in the style to which your average jogger might be accustomed and you quickly become unstuck. With your foot rubbing against the head of one of the nails, causing blistering to fragile Anglo-Saxon skin, there is a pain factor for the soft Westerner to work through.'

The Maasai, however, were adamant their shoes were perfect for covering long distances. 'They are very comfortable,' Isaya Lukumay told the paper. 'I wear them every day for looking after the cattle. They are good for chasing lions. We can run very fast in them. I have never tried your kind of running shoes. They don't look very good.' Shouldn't that be running away from lions?

Anyway, the proof, of course, is always in the pudding and dressed in traditional Maasai robes and their Michelin-inspired footwear, the six started the London Marathon and amazingly, four finished the race together in a time of five hours, 24 minutes and 47 seconds. Sadly Isaya was one of the two from the group who did not make it to the end, forced as he was to quit the race at the 12 mile (19.3km) mark because a ceremonial strapping on his leg had been tied too tightly and had affected his circulation. He was rushed to hospital but the next day he was back to cross the finishing line. 'It was very important for me to do this,' he beamed after completing the race. 'This is what I came to England for.'

And, maybe, for a welcome break from chasing all those lions.

FELICETTA AND THE FOX

ARIZONA, USA, 2008

If you're au fait with the Disney film *The Fox and the Hound*, Roald Dahl's book *Fantastic Mr Fox* or perhaps television's *The Basil Brush Show*, you're probably labouring under the impression that foxes are cute, cuddly creatures. Once you've read this particularly eye-watering tale of a runner's painful misfortune, you'll never see the furry little buggers in the same light again.

Our unfortunate jogger is Michelle Felicetta, a resident of Chino Valley in Arizona, who was running a 3 mile (4.8km) loop one morning around the base of Granite Mountain. She was 1 mile (1.6km) into her run when she spotted a fox in a clearing by the side of the track, and although she tried to give the vicious sod a wide berth, it became aggressive and began biting her leg.

Sadly for Michelle, this was only the beginning of the battle. She tried to grab her animal assailant by the neck and throw it off, but the fox really had its dander up by now and released its grip on her leg, sunk its teeth into her arm and steadfastly refused to let go.

To make matters even worse, Michelle was well aware that there was rabies in the area and her attacker would need to be tested for the disease, so she set off back to her car, running the mile back to her motor with the fox still stubbornly clamped to her bleeding forearm. Unsurprisingly she didn't quite dip under the magical four minutes for the distance, what with having a wild animal gnawing at her all the way, but once there she was able to prise the beast off and throw it into the boot of her car.

A desperate dash to the nearest hospital for treatment ensued, where she alerted the sheriff's department to the angry contents of her boot. An animal control officer was hastily summoned, but our ferocious fox wasn't quite finished yet, biting said officer as he attempted to get the animal out of the vehicle.

'This fox made eye contact with me and started walking towards me,' Michelle told local reporters after her ordeal. 'That's when I knew something was really wrong. I went to back up slowly, and as soon as I went to back up, it came and attacked my foot.'

Tests confirmed our carnivorous canine was indeed rabid and to add insult to injury, Michelle had to undergo a course of five painful vaccinations to ward against infection. The fate of our furious fox is not documented but we can probably safely assume that given its vicious behaviour the voracious critter may have been treated to 'a long sleep' rather than being quietly released back into the wild.

BREAST
ISN'T ALWAYS BEST
DEVON, 2008

Written by John Gray and first published in 1992, the book *Men Are from Mars, Women Are from Venus* was a big hit in the publishing world, musing as it did on the complexities of relationships and interaction between ladies and gentlemen. If you've not read it, the basic thematic thrust is that fellas like sitting in sheds and drinking beer (often simultaneously), while the girls prefer talking and sharing their feelings, and rarely shall the twain meet. There's also, if memory serves, something about sharing a mango but you get the general idea.

In the realms of running (not to mention other athletic activities), the male and female of the species also find themselves in opposite camps courtesy of a simple biological fact. Specifically, women runners have breasts to contend with while their male counterparts, unless they're exceedingly out of shape and have a Krispy Kreme loyalty card, do not.

As a result, women's quest to find sports bras with the required support, fit and level of comfort is as old as it is sometimes frustrating. Reducing 'the bounce' is big business and in 2008 female runners were heartened to hear boffins at the University of Plymouth were taking the problem very seriously indeed.

The vital research was conducted by the university's Breast Biometrics Team (who knew?) and involved a series of women taking to a treadmill with reflective sensors attached to their nipples, shoulders and hips. They were then asked to take a brisk two-minute jog in what more puerile minds dubbed the 'Boob Lab' while a computer measured, you know, how exactly their chests moved while running. It was all very scientific, so stop sniggering at the back.

There were some startling findings. Only 50 per cent of the total bounce was what was described as 'up and down', with 25 per cent attributed to 'side to side' movement, while the remaining quarter was identified as 'in and out', erm, undulations. The Plymouth team also revealed that one guinea pig had registered a sizeable 9⅔in (24.5cm) range of up and down shift.

'We're funded by various sports bra manufacturers, so I would never come out and recommend one particular brand,' head honcho Dr Joanna Scurr told the *Daily Mail*.

'But we're working to provide information that all brands can use. The only time I ever came across sniggers and giggles was when I was making a presentation at an international sports science conference last year. A room full of esteemed academics collapsed into embarrassed laughter every time I said the word "breasts". But I'm passionate about what I do and I usually convert people.'

The perfect sports bra of course remains a goal rather a reality but every new volunteer stepping onto the team's treadmill brings the dream one jog closer. If Dr Scurr and her colleagues do ever crack it, they've vowed to utilise their collective expertise to design a training vest for men that successfully manages to visibly reduce even the most pendulous of beer bellies.

A FESTIVE TOILET BREAK
LONDON, 2009

Christmas should be a magical time of the year for one and all. Probably slightly more magical for the kids seeing as they don't have to open (or pay) the MasterCard bill come January, or drive Auntie Doris back to Bournemouth on Boxing Day, but nevertheless the festive period is a time for merriment, mince pies and spending time with the family, whether you want to or not.

For one south London jogger in 2009, however, the Yuletide celebrations began in far from festive fashion as the poor chap found himself spending Christmas morning locked in a freezing public toilet block. And before you start casting any outrageous aspersions, the fella was doing absolutely nothing untoward.

Our runner was in fact innocently jogging around Dulwich Park in the capital on Christmas Eve, and at 4.30 in the afternoon at the end of his athletic exertions, he popped to the toilet to answer the call of the nature. Unfortunately while he was in there a council employee came along and, doubtless desperate to get to the pub for a little festive drinkie, promptly locked the door and made his exit stage left.

The jogger was stuffed. What with it being Christmas Eve and pitch dark, the park was unsurprisingly deserted and his cries for help went unheeded. He didn't have a mobile phone on him so he was unable to send out a telephonic

SOS and he was reluctantly forced to spend the next 17 hours shivering in the less-than-salubrious surroundings of a public toilet. There was at least hot water, a hand dryer and some spare bin liners to provide a semblance of warmth, but a night at The Savoy it was not.

It was not until 9.30 on the morning of the anniversary of the birth of the baby Jesus that our runner was finally released, rushing home to the bosom of his family to explain where the hell he had been all night. He had not, he hurriedly explained, been temping for Father Christmas.

'I'm very, very sorry about this incident and would like to offer my sincere apologies to the man involved and I can confirm that the council has offered compensation,' mumbled embarrassed Cllr Linda Manchester, executive member for community safety at Southwark Council, clearly expecting her P45 in the New Year. 'I'm glad that he wasn't harmed and that he was able to enjoy Christmas Day with his family. All our toilet buildings are checked every night before locking and so this should not have happened. The importance of making thorough checks of cubicles has been re-iterated to all members of the parks locking team. This is the first time anyone has been locked in the toilets and we do not envisage that it will ever happen again.'

So how much do you reckon being imprisoned in a public convenience on Christmas Eve is worth? It's sadly not as much as you think and our runner got a paltry £500 cheque from the council for his, ahem, inconvenience. He certainly wasn't feeling flush at all. Sorry, that's enough toilet gags for now.

ONLINE ILLEGALITY IN THE UK

UK, 2009

The world is run in a moral vacuum by avaricious, global multi-nationals that will stop at nothing in their inexhaustible corporate thirst for profit and power. That, you must understand, is not the opinion of anyone connected with this book, so Microsoft, Unilever, Audi, *et al*, you can stand the lawyers down. But it is, you know, what some other people we've never met think, and to be fair the world's biggest companies haven't always covered themselves in glory when it comes to how they treat the 'little people'.

A chastening case in point was in evidence in 2009 when an anonymous British runner sat down at his laptop and starting searching for some shiny new trainers. His extensive online search led our jogger to a rather fetching pair of Nikes, and after placing his order, he sat back and waited eagerly for his purchase to arrive.

What happened next was not what he had expected at all and rather than receiving a knock on the door from the chap from the Royal Mail or UPS, clutching a size nine-shaped box, our man was dismayed to receive a letter from the hounds from hell, aka Nike's legal department, informing him they were taking him to court for infringing the company's trademark. In layman's terms, our fella had inadvertently tried to buy a knock-off pair of trainers and Nike weren't having it.

Other runners who were caught up in the scam after the UK Border Agency had seized the hooky goods *en route* from China agreed to settle out of court, or simply offered no defence just to get Nike off their backs, but our chap was made of sterner stuff and argued it was far from a fair cop on the grounds he had clicked on 'Buy Item' in good faith and had absolutely no idea his order was not strictly kosher. Nike, however, refused to back down and the case went to court.

'I ordered training shoes over the Internet believing them to be authentic,' the man said. 'I had no idea they were counterfeit. I have never received any goods and will not be ordering any more.'

Unfortunately for him, ignorance proved to be a rather poor defence. 'Whether or not the Defendant believed the goods were authentic is irrelevant to the question of trademark infringement,' replied the judge without cracking a smile. 'Whether the goods are infringing goods or counterfeit goods is an objective question. The Defendant's state of mind does not matter. Equally the Defendant's state of mind is irrelevant to the question of importation.'

Things were looking bleak for our unlucky fella as the vultures circled but salvation was at hand when the judge summed up. Although he ruled in favour of Nike he conceded that maybe the company had, perhaps, overreacted just a little. 'It may be questioned whether the sledgehammer of these proceedings is necessary in order to crack this nut of this magnitude but Nike's representative explained, and I accept, that brand owners in this situation have no realistic alternative to enforcing their rights this way. Accordingly although this appears to be the smallest of cases, nevertheless the Claimant is entitled to bring proceedings.'

The upshot of it all was a bunch of lawyers got richer and our brave defendant had to undertake not to infringe Nike's trademark in the future, which really just meant not buying any dodgy Air Max off the World Wide Web. The lesson of the story is obviously that the lovely people at Nike are dedicated to delivering the very highest quality products possible and are just concerned that cheap, counterfeit trainers might hurt our toes. They are absolutely not, as some cynics who we don't know have suggested, big bullies with no heart.

HOP, SKIP AND A PUNCH
AUSTRALIA, 2010

If you've ever watched any of the 91 episodes of the seminal Australian TV series *Skippy the Bush Kangaroo*, you'll be labouring under the illusion that kangaroos are sweet, benign creatures who love nothing more than exposing sheep rustlers, thwarting gun-toting tearaways and saving crashed helicopter pilots.

No, in reality, kangaroos are giant, muscle-bound marsupials, which don't give a hoot about whether a dear old granny has sprained her ankle in the Outback. At the last count, kangaroos outnumbered people in Australia by roughly three to one, which means that there are 60 million plus of them loose Down Under, and while attacks on humans remain rare, with those kind of numbers it was only a matter of time before someone from the jogging fraternity had a run-in with one of Skippy's bad-tempered relatives.

The unfortunate chap who pulled the short straw was David Striegel, a real estate worker from Canberra, who was happily minding his own business as he ran up Mount Ainslie in the north-east suburbs of the city during his lunch break, only to suddenly find himself under attack, briefly unconscious and on the deck.

'I was jogging along, then I heard something, I didn't know what it was, coming at me from my left side,' David told reporters. 'I turned around and the kangaroo had a swipe at me, and scratched me across the face. Then it threw a punch, I guess, and collected me on my right side, so I'm sporting a black eye now. It appeared to come after me, so whether I disturbed what it was doing or it had a joey around, I wouldn't have a clue.

'The main thing people have been asking is whether I got a punch back on the roo. I can't even say that, because one punch and it put me to the floor. All my years of playing football and never a fight, and then I have a fight with a kangaroo.'

A 'fight' does rather imply a two-way contest in which two pugilists actually exchange blows, rather than one going down like a sack of spuds after one punch, but David was obviously still groggy and we'll let it pass.

Luckily for him, a passing motorist spotted him prostrate by the side of the road after the attack, and drove him to the local hospital, where he received a tetanus shot and was discharged. He was back at the work the next day, affording his waggish colleagues the opportunity to give David a new nickname. Which was of course 'Skippy'.

David is not the only runner to fall foul of an irate kangaroo Down Under. In 2008, a man in his fifties was out for a jog in the suburbs of Melbourne, when he was suddenly set upon by one of the marsupials and suffered a large gash to the head and injuries to his chest and hands. 'He was jogging near his home when he was attacked by a male kangaroo,' said the paramedic who treated our unlucky athlete. 'He managed to fight the kangaroo off and made his way to a neighbour's house, who called 000.'

The chief problem with evading potential kangaroo attacks is the buggers can reach a top speed of over 40mph (64.4km/h), so unless you happen to be Usain Bolt holidaying on the Gold Coast, your chances of outrunning your hairy assailant are minimal. As Mr Striegel can testify, they also pack a powerful punch. The best advice, should you come face to face with one on your morning run, is to walk very slowly in the opposite direction. And under no circumstances break into an impromptu rendition of 'Waltzing Matilda'. They really hate that.

TEENAGE TRICKS
YORKSHIRE, 2010

They say charity begins at home. Unfortunately, these days that often means an unsolicited cold call from the RSPCA or Amnesty International just as *Dancing on Ice* is about to start, but the point is we are a nation of givers, and without such altruistic financial instincts, a hell of a lot of kittens would be homeless and innocent people banged up.

The amount of money raised for charity by members of the running community over the years is huge. We're talking millions and millions here, and while it may irk miserly work colleagues when the office athlete thrusts yet another sponsorship form in their face, the cash generated for good causes is invaluable.

A whopping £53.2 million was raised by those who took part in the London Marathon in 2014, for example, making all the blisters and chafed nipples worthwhile, and since the inaugural race in the capital in 1981, somewhere north of £700 million has been raked in by runners and their generous sponsors.

Residents in Hull certainly believed they were doing the right thing when they signed on the dotted line in 2010 after they were approached by three teenagers who asked for sponsorship for their attempt to complete a 10 mile (16.1km) run in aid of Breast Cancer Care. Unfortunately all was not as it seemed, and when the Old Bill questioned the three lads about a missing bicycle, it emerged that their 'run' was a shameless scam designed to line their own pockets.

Punishment obviously had to be meted out, but rather than bother with all the paperwork and solicitors, the local bobby who'd felt their collar decided the miscreants would complete the 10 miles after all. To compound their misery they were forced to run their penance at 10 o'clock on a Saturday morning, a time when all self-respecting teenagers are still festering in their pits.

'These lads are not bad lads really,' insisted PC Andy White as he marched the monosyllabic and bleary-eyed offenders to the start line. 'They come from good families and what they did obviously got out of hand. It is lads being lads and I didn't think the courts would have been the appropriate punishment. I think this will teach them a better lesson, they have done wrong and they know it.

'If they had been through the court system they would have had a criminal record which could have affected their chances of work in the future. I thought that would be over-the-top for something they have done at a young age.

'I am not interested in targets and figures, that is not what neighbourhood policing should be about. We decided to use this final warning as an opportunity to give the three lads a chance to earn back the money they obtained. We invited some of the victims along who paid the boys the money to be present at the start of the run.'

An unconventional punishment indeed. After crossing the finishing line, out trio of scammers were taken to the local nick and received formal cautions for their misbehaviour and everybody agreed to move on. The teenagers were lucky in one respect though and quietly thanked their lucky stars that they hadn't claimed to be running a marathon.

BACK IN TIME
GEORGIA, USA, 2010

Running is all about going fast. Regardless of the distance, all runners strive for the fastest time possible and if you ever spy a runner out and about without a watch on their wrist, you can safely assume they've just been mugged. The hours, minutes and seconds are what really matter.

World record times are of course the preserve of only the finest athletes on the planet, the men and women at the very top of their game, and while a decent amateur for example might target 25 minutes for a 5K (3$^1/_8$ miles), they're not going to get anywhere near the 12 minutes and 37.35 seconds clocked by Ethiopia's Kenenisa Bekele in May 2004, which still stands as the fastest ever time over the distance.

Or could they? Is there a way, without the clandestine use of a motorbike or some seriously strong performance enhancing drugs, an average runner could in fact eclipse Kenny's record time and complete a 5K in under 12 minutes? The answer is yes. Sort of. Provided you're not hung up on the concept of time as a linear progression. And know how to put a clock back.

The setting for our improbable world record attempt is the city of Kennesaw in Georgia, USA. The race is called the 'Impossible 5K' and since it was first held in 2010 virtually all of those who have entered the event have been smashing Bekele's milestone.

What initially sets the 'Impossible 5K' apart from most other races is the start time – 1.50a.m. The real clincher, however, is the fact that it is held on the night that Daylight Saving Time begins in the States and that means the clocks go backwards while you're still out on the course (a two-lap loop around the local shopping mall). That in turn means if you do complete the race in, say, 25 minutes, you cross the finishing line at 1.15a.m. And that means you've *technically* just run your 5K in *minus* 35 minutes. Forget Kenenisa Bekele, even *Doctor Who* can't do that.

Sadly the International Association of Athletics Federations have taken rather a dim view of those 'Impossible 5K' runners who have claimed new world records, arguing they're clearly mental, and have stubbornly refused to recognise their incredible times. Similarly *Guinness World Records* have not deigned to legitimise their efforts either.

The organisers of the race don't care one iota. They can go back in time and have hastily convened a lottery syndicate.

THE EVIL ELEMENTS
IOWA, USA, 2010

Checking the weather forecast before heading out for a run is never a bad idea. The elements can be extremely fickle and if you're out on the open road, a few miles from home, and Mother Nature suddenly decides she's going to throw a climatic wobbler, you can find yourself rather exposed.

And so it was for four unfortunate members of the Grinnell College Cross Country team in Iowa when they strode out for a training run but ended up in hospital looking like they had just endured a two-week holiday in a particularly vicious medieval torture chamber.

The quartet were initially jogging happily along the rural roads of the Hawkeye State but storm force winds that reached up to 75mph (121km/h) suddenly blew up as if from nowhere, buffeting our hapless students. Worse was to follow when the heavens opened and the four were battered by hailstones the size of golf balls.

The freezing barrage was agony but there was no cover anywhere and the runners' only option was to jump into a ditch by the side of the road in a desperate bid to avoid the worst of the icy deluge. The ditch provided scant shelter and they were quickly forced to abandon the trench as it began to fill with water and flood. Back out in the open, they were once again pounded relentlessly from on high.

Things were looking bleak for our quartet but salvation was finally at hand when good Samaritan Pat Crawford and her husband happened to drive by. They were confronted by a disturbing scene of four distraught young men covered from head to toe in big red impact marks and cuts all over their bodies from the hailstones. They bundled the dishevelled group into the back of their car and headed straight to hospital, where the youngsters were treated for suspected broken ribs among their other painful injuries.

'There was a kid in the road looking like he was flagging things down,' Pat said. 'You could tell he was a runner because he had the running shorts on, he was barefooted, and he looked pretty beat up. They thought it was a tornado. A lot of us thought it was a tornado. So they laid in the ditch, which was a good idea but they were just getting the tar beat out of them and the ditches were filling with water, so they knew they couldn't stay there. It was unbelievable. I've never seen a human body that looked that beat up.'

Pat took a series of pictures on her phone to record just how severe the students' injuries were, and should you wish to view in graphic detail the pain wrought by Mother Nature on the poor lads, a quick search of the World Wide Web will oblige. The boys were evidently a little embarrassed by their experience and asked to remain anonymous but the local media were still happy enough, the incident providing the opportunity to run classic tabloid headlines such as 'Hurts Like Hail', 'Hail on Earth' and, the rather less pithy, 'Stupid Students' Severe Storm Scare Shocker'.

THE NEED FOR POST MORTEM SPEED

UTAH, USA, 2011

It's impossible to escape zombies these days. Not literally obviously because they don't actually exist, but whether it be on television, the big screen or on your PS4, the undead are everywhere. Jokes about the House of Lords can be inserted here at your pleasure.

Everyone knows how to kill a zombie – a sharp blow or bullet to the head, job done – but a fierce debate still rages over the really big question about the undead. Can zombies run? It divides fans of the genre right down the middle.

The early cinematic zombies brought to us by the famed director George A. Romero in the seminal *Night of the Living Dead* and its sequels were exceedingly slow and cumbersome. They'd happily have you for lunch if they could catch you, but as long as you kept moving and didn't get cornered, your life expectancy was pretty good. Things changed with films like *28 Days Later* and *World War Z* in which the undead suddenly started doing passable impressions of Usain Bolt and the argument about the rapidity or otherwise of the reanimated began.

'I do have rules in my head of what's logical and what's not,' Romero once said in an interview. 'I don't think zombies can run. Their ankles would snap. I prefer these plodding, lumbering guys from whom you can easily escape unless you injure yourself somehow and are too stupid to do the right thing. That's just more fun for me.'

All this is relevant to us because one of the most recent phenomena in the running world is the zombie-themed race, and should you choose to enter one, the relative speeds of the human and undead competitors are really rather important. One of the first of these slightly macabre events was the 'Night of the Running Dead' race over in the States, first staged in 2010 in Salt Lake City, where entrants can choose whether to complete the 5K ($3^1/8$ mile) course as either the living or the undead. The humans get a two-minute head start and must get to the finishing line without being nibbled.

And here's the bone of contention. If you're in the Romero camp and hold that zombies are only capable of a pedestrian pace, you're not going to take kindly to being chased down by an undead entrant who'd give Seb Coe a run for his money. Equally, if you opt to enter as zombie, and faithfully adhere to the Romero school of perambulation, you're never going to catch a bloody soul.

There's a plethora of undead athletic events out there these days – the Zombie Evacuation Race, the Zombie Race, the Run For Your Lives 5K, the Zombie Survival Run and the Zombie Apocalypse 5K to name but five – but the whole 'can zombies run?' debate is yet to be satisfactorily resolved.

TERROR AT THE POST OFFICE

CALIFORNIA, USA, 2011

The choice of running kit these days is dizzying. In ye olden times it was simple – trainers, shorts, vest, job done – but today joggers are confronted with a myriad of (invariably expensive) options and choices and it is increasingly common for runners to spend more time going through their wardrobes selecting an 'outfit' than they actually do out on the road.

Should you wear the long-sleeved base layer or the short-sleeved zipped singlet? The baggy trail running shorts or the breathable mesh speed shorts? Trainer socks or knee-lengthers? And let's not even get started with the sheer volume of footwear currently on the market. It's an absolute minefield out there.

One runner who definitely got his sartorial choices very, very wrong indeed was American student Long Hoang, who decided to pop out for a brisk jog near his apartment in San Jose in 2011, but unwittingly sparked a major terror alert, the evacuation of petrified postal staff and the deployment of the local bomb squad.

The problem started when Long received some misdirected mail. A keen runner, he decided to return the package to his nearest Post Office while out on his daily run, and dressed appropriately. Unfortunately 'appropriately' for Long meant a gas mask over his face and what looked very much like a bulletproof vest.

We'll get to the reasons for his bizarre outfit in due course but suffice to say Long headed out looking not unlike Bane from *Batman* and proceeded to shove the aforementioned parcel into a mailbox. He was spotted by a passer-by who was rather understandably alarmed by what he saw, assumed he was trying to blow up the Post Office or at the very least poison the staff with some toxin, and alerted the authorities.

Long was oblivious to the panic he'd just caused and jogged happily off, while behind him the Fire Department's hazardous materials unit was called in, the San Jose bomb squad hastily deployed and 150 employees and customers bundled into the back of the building for safe keeping. A robot was sent in and after four hours the lockdown was lifted when the fearless automaton blew up the suspect package.

Phew, what a palaver! The first thing that Long knew of the chaos he had caused was when CCTV images of the 'bomber' appeared on the local news and his friends began to call and text, and like a good little soldier, he handed himself into the coppers.

So why the hell did he look like an off-the-peg terrorist while out for what should have been a simple jog? Long explained that he was following an exercise regime called CrossFit, and that the mask was to restrict the flow of oxygen and so simulate high-altitude training, while inside the pockets of the vest there was nothing more sinister than some weights. 'The guy said he was wearing a cardio mask,' San Jose police Sergeant Jason Dwyer told the local media. 'It was his cardio day and he was trying to lose weight.'

Gotcha. The boys in blue weren't happy but had to concede he hadn't actually committed any crime and sent him on his way. 'Totally big misunderstanding, totally unintended on my part,' Long said as he beat a hasty retreat, avoiding the gaze of the snipers with itchy trigger fingers. 'I won't do anything like this ever again.'

Two footnotes here. Firstly the package at the centre of the furore was full of innocent calendars. Secondly, and this is absolutely true, Long revealed he had lost 20lb (9.1kg) in 12 weeks on the CrossFit programme, so however ridiculous he may have looked, and regardless how close he came to a little holiday in Guantanamo Bay, the ends really did justify the means.

A YEAR TO REMEMBER
BELGIUM AND THE WORLD, 2011

There have been some riveting books written about running, not least this very tome of course, but it's safe to say the diary of Belgian athlete Stefaan Engels for the year 2011 is not one of them. Brevity precludes a full reproduction here of what amounts to literary Prozac but a little taster should give you a sense of the wide-ranging subject matter:

5 February: Ran a marathon. *6 February:* Jogged 26.2 miles [42.2km]. *7 February:* Marathon. *8 February:* Long run. 26.2 miles maybe. *9 February:* Left note for milkman. Ran 42.195km. *10 February:* Another marathon. *11 February:* Overslept. Ran. Just over 26 miles [41.8km].

And so it continues, uninterrupted and unabated, right through to February 2012. Yes, that's right, Stefaan ran 365 consecutive marathons in 365 days. That's 9,569 miles (15,399km) in the calendar year without a solitary day off. Whatever the weather. In seven different countries. Imagine how many pairs of trainers he got through.

Stefaan first got the 'endurance bug' competing in Iron Man triathlons, but after setting a world record as the only man to complete 20 of them in a calendar year, he turned his attention to marathon running. One evidently was not enough and the seeds of his year-long challenge were sown.

He set off on 5 February from his hometown of Ghent and over the subsequent 12 months visited Portugal, Canada, Mexico, the UK and the USA, as he clocked up mile after mile after mile, finishing in Barcelona with the Carretera de les Aigües race. Stefaan averaged four hours per day on the road to complete each marathon while his fastest time for the 26.2 miles was two hours and 56 minutes.

'After running 20 triathlons in one year, I was not ready to go back to normal life,' he explained. 'I also wanted to inspire people by showing that if I could run a marathon a day for an entire year, that anyone could run or bike a little each day or do something about their weight problem.

'I recover quickly. I don't run fast and my heartbeat is slow, below 100 if I run 10km [6.2 miles], but it is more a mental story. The problem was thinking about running a marathon every day. I just told myself to run that day and did not think about the next day or next week.

'I don't regard my marathon year as torture. It's more like a regular job. I am running just as Joe Average goes to work on Monday morning, whether or not he feels like it. I don't always feel like running but when I am done, I take a shower, have some physiotherapy for an hour, and that wraps up my day.

'There were a lot of moments when I thought "today, I won't finish". One of the hardest moments was in Mexico City after a long flight, the altitude and I had gotten sick from eating something, and I thought "what am I doing here?"'

It's a question most of us would have asked every single day for the entire, agonising year but Stefaan admitted his great adventure was inspired by a childhood diagnosis of asthma and the strict instructions of doctors not to get involved in sport. Nothing if not a stubborn bugger then, and his feat eclipsed the previous record of 150 consecutive marathons, set by Spaniard Ricardo Abad Martinez in 2009.

More importantly his exploits made the ever popular

party game, 'Name Ten Famous Belgians', just that little bit easier. Eddie Merckx obviously, The Smurfs of course, Jean-Claude Van Damme is from Brussels, that painter, the tennis player, erm, hang on, no sorry, that's it.

CENTURION SINGH

CANADA, 2011

It was Muhammad Ali who once said, 'Age is whatever you think it is, you are as old as you think you are.' It's not quite as catchy as his whole 'float like a butterfly, sting like a bee, the hands can't hit what the eyes can't see' routine, but Muhammad was certainly ahead of his time in championing the potential of OAPs everywhere.

Whether the incredible Fauja Singh was a big fan of Ali in his prime is unclear. He's easily old enough to remember both the Thrilla in Manila and indeed the Rumble in the Jungle, but this book is about running not boxing, and it is Fauja and his remarkable centenarian exploits that shall take us forward here.

Fauja was born in India in April 1911. In April 2011 he celebrated, wait for it, his one hundredth birthday but, even more significantly, in October 2011 he entered and completed the Toronto Waterfront Marathon to become the first person in history with three figures on the clock to run 26 miles, 385 yards. It took him eight hours, 11 minutes and six seconds to get the job done, but when you're 100 years old and you'd set yourself a target of nine hours, you're allowed to take your time. Much to their chagrin, he actually outpaced five other entrants with his 3,850th-place finish.

'Beating his original prediction, he's overjoyed,' said Harmander Singh, Fauja's trainer and interpreter, after he crossed the finishing line. 'Just before we came around the final corner, he said "achieving this will be like getting married again".'

An uplifting story indeed, but an unwelcome twist came not long after when it emerged the revered *Guinness World Records* would not officially recognise him as either the first centenarian to complete a marathon, or even the oldest person to run the distance. As so often in such things, there was a problem with the ruddy paperwork.

More specifically it was Fauja's birth certificate. More specifically than that, it was the absence of his birth certificate. 'We would love to give him the record,' said Craig Glenday, the *GWR* editor-in-chief. 'We'd love to say this is a true Guinness World Record, but the problem is there is just no evidence. We can only accept official birth documents created in the year of the birth. Anything else is really not very useful to us.'

Bugger. Fauja may have been born in India, but moved to Blighty in 1992, and his British passport listed his year of birth as 1911. He had his one hundredth birthday card from the Queen, and even a letter from Indian government officials explaining the reason he didn't have a birth certificate was because they were not issued in the country in 1911, but it was all to no avail and *GWR* were not for turning.

The response from the Fauja camp was surprisingly magnanimous. 'I think it's important to everybody who's over a certain age, because it inspires them and allows them to think "yes, it is possible",' said his old mate Harmander Singh. 'However, the fact remains that the *Guinness World Records* has its rules, and I think they are quite right to have them.'

For the record, Fauja finally hung up his trainers in 2013, a couple of months short of his one hundred and second birthday, and in 2015 he was awarded the British Empire Medal for his services to sport and charity in the New Year's Honours List. It's customary for recipients of such awards at the palace to genuflect before receiving their gongs but Fauja was spared that on the grounds that his knees were absolutely knackered.

GO FASTER WITH FAST FOOD

CALIFORNIA, USA, 2011

'You are what you eat' is a mantra beloved of marathon runners, and whenever a race approaches, thoughts inevitably turn to what to have for dinner the night before. Easily digestible carbohydrates are the order of the day and marathoners chow down on their pre-match meal with a relish matched only by their zeal for talking about trainers.

The BBC website recommends a dish of pasta, bacon, mushrooms and pesto the night before your 26 miles, 385 yards. Yummy. The *Runner's World* website advocates a chicken burrito with rice, corn salsa and black beans. Delicious. *The Guardian* champions rigatoni, butternut squash and pancetta. Bravo, chef.

None of them, however, suggest nipping down to the nearest McDonald's, which brings us neatly to an American fella by the name of Joe D'Amico who decided that his preparations for the Los Angeles Marathon in 2011 would include eating only what he could purchase from the fast food behemoth. Yes, that's right, Joe decided to eat nothing but McDonald's for 30 days before running in LA.

'I've been eating McDonald's since I was a kid,' Joe explained. 'In a way I've been practising for this my whole life. I can do it because I'm running 100 miles [161km] a week. I've been feeling really good. My wife thinks I'm crazy, but I love McDonald's and I love running and this is a great way to combine them both.'

Now before you dismiss Joe as a *complete* nut job it's worth noting that some of the McDonald's menu was, well, off the menu and he refused to eat Big Macs or order large fries, and for the record, he breakfasted on Egg McMuffins, while lunch was two grilled chicken wraps, *three-quarters* of a bag of fries and a large Coke. His evening meal was two hamburgers and more Coke followed by a hot fudge sundae or chocolate chip cookies.

The more cynical among you will of course already harbour suspicions that this was no more than a PR stunt cooked up by McDonald's in an attempt to give their fare some kind of healthy veneer but 'McRunner' (as Joe was inevitably dubbed) was adamant in his blog – 'Confessions of a Drive-Thru Runner' – that there were absolutely no backhanders going on.

So how did Joe get on in what was the fifteenth marathon of his career? Remarkably he crossed the finishing line in twenty-ninth place, in a time of two hours, 36 minutes and 13 seconds, 30 seconds quicker than his previous best.

'I couldn't ask for a better run on a tough course in difficult conditions,' he said after the race. 'If you make good choices and better choices more often than not, you're going to have good results. There's diet, there's exercise, there's stress. There's a lot of things. That's something I try to tell people to keep in mind. Don't focus on one aspect, look at things as a whole. From day one, I received such positive feedback and encouragement from friends, family and even those I never met. That made me realize that I could provide more than just a little entertainment and inspiration. I could actually make a difference.'

It's highly debatable what difference Joe's bizarre stunt actually made. The number of McDonald's' customers probably went up as a result, but unless you've sold your soul and work in advertising, increasing McChicken sandwich sales is hardly an epitaph many would aspire to.

MENACE IN THE SKIES

SOUTH WALES, 2011

Have you seen the Alfred Hitchcock film *The Birds*? Absolutely terrifying it is, the good folk of a small American town besieged by killer seagulls, vicious sparrows and disgruntled crows, and forced to run for their lives. Luckily it's only cinematic fiction and unless it's the old pirate-parrot combo, birds tend to give people a wide berth.

Or that's what geologist Alan Rosier thought when he went out for a training run in Pontywaun in South Wales in 2011 and found himself under an unexpected aerial attack from one of our more irate feathered friends. His assailant was a buzzard and, as with all large birds of prey, it was capable of doing serious damage and left Alan with a deep gash.

'I've never seen anything like it. It was a real shock to see a bird attack like that. It just missed me on its first attempt, so it circled back round for a second try but just missed again. I carried on with my run but on the return leg the buzzard finally caught up with me. It hit me in the back of the head and caused a gash. I kept on running just to get away.

'It was very surprising and I won't be running along that track again for a few weeks. I was lucky to escape more serious injury and don't want to be dive-bombed again. I see the birds every time I run but they are usually high in the sky and I didn't think I was in any danger from them. But from now on you can be sure I'm going to keep a wary eye skywards just in case.'

So why had the buzzard gone rogue? Sadly Bill Oddie was not available to comment, but thankfully the Forestry Commission's Clive Davies was on hand to offer his expert ornithological view. 'Buzzards are very territorial but we have never heard of an incident like this before in Wales,' he said. 'Usually they only attack other birds. They nest from April until July and normally [their chicks] would have flown the nest by now. It may have been a young bird which was startled.'

There may though be a more sinister explanation. Birds of prey may in fact be massing in some kind of coordinated avian coup against the running community. In 2012, for example, teenager Connor Bower suffered whiplash while out jogging in South Shields after he was knocked to the ground by a disgruntled eagle owl, while a buzzard was the culprit again when Darren Sheppard was attacked out on his run in Derby in 2015. In the same year marathoner Paul Bray needed three stitches to his ear after falling foul of the attentions of a hawk, while over in the States, joggers in Oregon were subjected to a series of unprovoked attacks by a barred owl.

What the hell is going on? The evidence that birds of prey have got a serious problem with runners is stacking up but it remains a mystery what exactly has ruffled their feathers. Maybe Mr Hitchcock knew something we don't.

INDECENT IN CINCINNATI

OHIO, USA, 2011

It's generally a good idea not to mess with the police in the USA. The boys in blue over the pond are notorious tough nuts, they carry guns and when you think about how much coffee they drink on a daily basis, it's hardly surprising they're invariably on the edge.

A chap called Brett Henderson should have given all that some thought before he entered the 'Flying Pig Marathon' in Cincinnati in 2011. If he had, he might have avoided jail, a criminal conviction and a lifetime ban from the race.

Brett's first crime was his failure to cough up the $110 entry fee. That oversight, however, paled in comparison to his inability to find a pair of shorts that fit him properly and before the race he was forced to borrow a pair from his dad. These sadly were not the right size at all and kept falling down, and when Brett was spotted out on the course by Cincinnati's finest, he was stark naked. What had happened to his running vest is a mystery.

The long arm of the law pulled up alongside Brett and suggested he come with them. He refused and carried on running. The police insisted he stop to 'have a little chat' but no dice, and after one last attempt to politely preserve public decency, they shot him right there and then with a Taser and bundled him into the back of a car. He had been warned.

Brett was subsequently charged with public indecency and obstructing official business but our naked athlete pleaded not guilty and was unrepentant about his antics. 'This is something that happens and is tolerated in the running culture, along with runners who sometimes urinate or defecate during a race,' he said. 'Shouldn't that be considered indecent exposure, too, if what I did was indecent? In fact, running naked was encouraged in a marathon I ran in San Francisco, so I don't know why this was such a big deal.'

It was your John Thomas flapping all about the place, Brett, your John Thomas. And the fact Cincinnati is considerably more conservative than San Francisco.

His mum Lee waded into the furore, insisting her little boy had only carried on running after his dad's shorts had come off because he was determined to finish the race, but once again it was unclear why he wasn't wearing anything on the upper half of his body.

Brett was in court within two weeks of his arrest and was convicted of public indecency and disorderly conduct. He was sentenced to 80 hours of community service, ordered to retrospectively pay the $110 entry fee and told never to darken the Flying Pig's door ever again. 'This behaviour is immature and selfish,' the judge said. 'If you want attention, do something constructive. It's not funny.'

Brett pleaded for a second chance and promised he'd remain fully clothed if he was allowed to run again. And pigs might fly was the general response.

MICKEY AND THE MARATHON MADAM

CALIFORNIA, USA, 2012

The Walt Disney Company loves families. Absolutely adores them in fact. True, their theme parks, saccharine-sweet TV shows and films and ubiquitous merchandising outlets are primarily targeted at kids rather than adults, but seven-year-olds don't tend to have that much hard currency to spend, and without the deep pockets of mum and dad, Disney might make a few millions less in annual profit. Heaven forbid.

Everything in the Disney world has to be squeaky clean, lest the aforementioned families are offended and take their wallets and purses home, and in 2012 the corporate suits behind Mickey Mouse *et al* had a real headache on their hands that threatened to drag the company's name through the mud.

The problem concerned the annual Disney Half Marathon. 'It's the moment you've been training for,' promises the blurb on the website. 'Your 13.1 mile [21.1km] run on a magical course in the Happiest Race on Earth takes you through Disney California Adventure Park … You'll complete your Disneyland Half Marathon race with an exciting finish near the Disneyland Hotel. It all adds up to miles of smiles, unforgettable memories, and a perfect ending to a magical Disneyland Half Marathon Weekend.' Do you think they mentioned Disney enough?

For the 2012 race Disney invited a former Olympic athlete

by the name of Suzy Favor Hamilton to add a bit of glamour and sparkle to the event. She had competed for the USA at the 1992, 1996 and 2000 Games in the 1500m, and as a mother herself, she was on message with the target audience. Athlete? Check. Kids? Definitely. Book her now. Suzy duly accepted the gig as the 'face of the race', ran about a bit, posed for photos and cashed her cheque.

The problems started later in the year when it emerged our Suzy had been earning a bit of extra money as, ahem, a 'professional girlfriend'. A gentleman's intimate companion. A lady of the night (although she did apparently accept daytime bookings). Yes, Suzy has been plying the oldest profession in the world to generate a few additional dollars.

Her exposure as an escort was very public indeed and the Disney executives who had booked her for the half marathon were ashen when the news broke. It definitely wasn't the wholesome family vibe they were desperate to create.

Suzy however was unapologetic. 'I'm owning up to what I did,' she said. 'I would not blame anybody except myself. Everybody in this world makes mistakes. I made a huge mistake. Huge. But I'm not about to hide in shame. I'm here, perfectly willing to remain in the public eye.'

Disney of course were not willing to remain associated with her in any shape or form and promptly withdrew their invitation to Suzy to come along to the half marathon in 2013. Mickey Mouse was said to be philosophical about the furore but Donald Duck was spitting feathers.

SAM'S SILVER SCREEN RESCUE

LONDON, 2012

The stars of Hollywood generally get a pretty bad press. Their critics claim movie actors are pampered, overpaid and obnoxious, and should rank somewhere on a par with management consultants and parking wardens if the fabric of society breaks down, it all goes a bit *Lord of the Flies* and we have to decide who's first up in front of the firing squad.

There are though exceptions to every rule. For reasons that have never become entirely clear, it's illegal to say a bad word about Tom Hanks even though he was responsible for *The Da Vinci Code* making it to the big screen, while the fact Angelina Jolie hasn't made a decent film since 1999 is rarely mentioned on account of all her great work for charidee.

There is one big name from Hollywood, however, who is genuinely worthy of mention in dispatches after his quick thinking saved the life of a jogger in 2012, a rescue act that Messrs Willis, Statham or Diesel could only dream of in real life.

Our lucky runner was Sam Dempster, who was nearing the end of his 4 mile (6.4km) trot in London's Hyde Park, when he suddenly suffered a cardiac arrest. Poor Sam hit the tarmac hard face-first and began to froth at the mouth, and was badly in need of urgent medical attention if he was going to come through. Mercifully, a call from a passer-by summoned an ambulance in the nick of time and Sam, a mere pup at the age of 27, was saved. The shock of suffering a heart attack was almost matched by the subsequent surprise when he found out who'd dialled 999.

'I am so grateful to him for calling an ambulance,' Sam said from his hospital bed. 'If it wasn't for him, I might not be here. When my friends told me Dustin Hoffman had saved my life, I thought it was a joke and they were trying to cheer me up. Now I know it's true, it still feels surreal.

'He is my new favourite actor. I don't know his films well, but my friends have bought me *Rain Man* so I'll watch that. I have no memory of what happened. The paramedics told me I had been saved by him. It's unbelievable. I can't wait to get running around the park again.'

According to one of the paramedics who attended the scene, our Dustin, who just happened to be walking back to his house in London, didn't merely make the life-saving phone call.

'Mr Hoffman stood around for the whole resuscitation which lasted for about 15 minutes,' said Martin Macarthur. 'He was making quiet comments throughout. It makes the job quite notable to be given a hand-over from a Hollywood A-lister. It doesn't happen every day.

'Any time you turn up the witnesses are the most important people because they can tell you exactly what has happened before the collapse. And there was Dustin Hoffman. We got there very quickly and it was obvious Sam was in cardiac arrest. He was taking dying breaths so we had to act fast. Dustin had turned him over on to his back, which was really useful and would have assisted in making sure his airway was open.

'He was really interested in what was happening but did not interfere in any way. Once we had resuscitated Sam, Dustin came over and said "Great job, guys". We get thanked a lot in our job but it is something a bit special coming from the man himself.'

Quite, although the ambulance crew did rather spoil the

moment when they accidentally picked up Dustin's iPod, wallet, umbrella and sunglasses, believing they belonged to Sam, and made off with them. What on earth a jogger would be doing with an umbrella is a perfectly reasonable question but the items were returned to our hero of the hour when they realised their mistake.

The incident of course gave the media a golden opportunity to reference Hoffman's role in the acclaimed 1976 flick *Marathon Man*. 'Marathon Man Saves Jogger'. Geddit? 'Hollywood Heavyweight Hoffman's Heart Attack Heroics in Hyde Park' would have worked too. Not quite as pithy though.

BLINDED BY THE LIGHT
TYNE AND WEAR, 2012

There's something magical about Hi-Vis jackets. It doesn't matter who you are, just pop on a fluorescent singlet and random members of the public will automatically assume you the man, someone with authority, the person in charge of the situation. Not even the most cleverest of scientists can explain why a DayGlo, Hi-Vis jacket has such an effect, but not unlike the 'One Ring' in *The Hobbit*, he who wears the brightly coloured tunic shall be the master of all they survey.

The mystical power of the jacket was perfectly illustrated in 2012 at the staging of the Town Moor Memorial 10K in Newcastle upon Tyne. The runners were all in position, the course had been cleared and everyone was under starter's orders. What could possibly go wrong? Except, that is, a cyclist out for an innocent ride. A cyclist wearing a Hi-Vis jacket of course.

'Runners at today's event will be aware the race had to be restarted due to the lead runners taking an incorrect route as they approached the lake,' said the organisers. 'As a result most athletes ran around 800m [½ mile] before they were called back to start the race again.

"This was due to a member of the public entering the course on a bicycle just before the starting gun was sounded. The cyclist was dressed in fluorescent clothing and as the leading group of runners ran closer to him they mistook him to be a race official and mistakenly followed him to the right instead of carrying straight on. We apologise for any inconvenience caused and will take steps in future events to ensure this does not happen again.'

Told you, people will follow a fluorescent jacket to the ends of the earth. It's the human equivalent of the magpie's obsession with anything shiny.

The restaged race was won by a Morpeth man called Ian Hudspith who was extremely relieved not to have been penalised for our cyclist's impromptu appearance. 'I had not ran the race before so I just followed the leaders and lo and behold we were told by a marshal we were going the wrong way,' he said. 'When we eventually got back on track I was in about fiftieth place and well down on the leaders who had gone the right way. It was shortly after that it was decided to halt the race and start all over again, which was the sensible thing to do and as far as I could gather everyone accepted the decision.'

The identity of the errant cyclist remains a mystery to this day. Race security should have stopped the accidental incursion onto the course, but since the rider was wearing a fabled fluorescent Hi-Vis jacket, they quite understandably assumed they were in charge and immediately waved them through.

A MURDER OF CROWS
COLORADO, USA, 2012

The great dogs versus cats debate has been raging ever since man domesticated both beasts and it's an argument that tends to get people jolly hot under the collar as they passionately extol the respective virtues of each animal as pets. Dog owners insist canines are the more loyal and loveable while cat lovers are adamant felines are more intelligent and independent.

We're probably not going to settle the age-old argument here but what we can say without fear of offending either camp is that dogs have rather cornered the market when it comes to running. More specifically, canines are without question the go-to animal when people fancy some company as they embark on a brisk 5K, and while cats may be an inexhaustible source of comedy clips on YouTube, not even the most besotted feline fan would argue that they're natural running partners for us humans.

A cautionary tale to illustrate the point comes from the town of Lafayette in Colorado and concerns a chap called Seth Franco, a 19-year-old student at the local high school, who landed himself in hot water with the authorities after heading out for a run with his kitty in tow.

It was, by all accounts, a beautiful day and Seth was keen for his cat Stella to enjoy the fine weather. He also wanted to go for a jog around the local lake and, ignoring all the aforementioned rules about cats being useless running companions, he popped a lead on Stella and set off. It was all going swimmingly, until Stella's little legs began to tire under the hot sun and Seth decided to let her rest up, tying her up to a rock underneath a tree as he continued to pound around the lake.

Unfortunately Stella's presence rather annoyed the local bird population and she was mobbed by a murder of crows (which just happens to be the ominous collective noun for crows). Fellow joggers had to intervene to save her from losing one of her nine lives and someone phoned the Old Bill, who promptly felt Seth's collar after informing him it was against city law to tie up an animal in a public space. The fact that Stella had also nearly been pecked to death didn't help his case and he was fined and summoned to appear in court on a charge of animal cruelty.

'I'm more of a dog person but this cat is so cool that I just took her in and take care of her,' Seth explained after his brush with the law. 'She was tied up to a tree behind school with a note that said, "I need a new home". I just care a lot about her. I guess more than the average person does. I love her.

'I thought, maybe before work I can go run the lake and the cat can come with me. She ran about 45 per cent of the way and then it was so hot she started panting real bad. They were yelling at me, telling me I abuse my animal. I did not intentionally abuse my animal. If anything, I just take care of it. They kind of just told me it was common sense to not tie an animal up. But don't abandon or hurt or abuse your animals or leave them tied up while you go jogging because you'll get in trouble.'

Lesson learned, Seth was eventually allowed to take Stella home with strict instructions not to take her running with him again. If cats could talk, which they can't, she would have probably muttered something along the lines of 'Thank Christ for that'.

A FLYING FRIEND IN THE SKY

AUSTRALIA, 2012

Written by Alan Sillitoe in 1959 and famously turned into a film three years later, *The Loneliness of the Long Distance Runner* is the story of a Borstal boy's mental (if not literal) escape from the anguish of incarceration through running. It is not, despite its title, a thesis on why serious joggers struggle to make friends.

The title does though take us neatly onto the subject of companionship in the sport and, more specifically, what to do when there's no one else around to run with and you suddenly realise you've neglected to buy a dog. The point is that people often prefer to run in pairs.

Step forwards the 'Joggobot', a potential answer to the prayers of reluctant solitary runners everywhere, and further proof that for every modern dilemma, someone will come up with a technological solution. The brainchild of a team of boffins from the Royal Melbourne Institute of Technology in Australia, a prototype 'Joggobot' was first unveiled in 2012 and was a drone, or more specifically a quadcopter, which was designed to fly in front of lonely joggers who could control the flying robot's pace and altitude with a smartphone app.

A camera fixed to the 'Joggobot' locked onto a blue and orange marker on the runner's vest to ensure man and machine stayed together and it came with two settings – 'companion mode', which saw the robot move at the same speed as its human master, and 'coach mode', which allowed the quadcopter to set a more challenging pace.

'Social joggers have partners they can run with,' explained Chad Toprak, one of the design team. 'But sometimes they aren't available, so the next best thing could be a robot. It's a really unique feeling to be running with it. The coach mode basically tries to push you to your limits. It flies in front of you at a very fast speed and you've got to try and catch up. I've tried running and sprinting with it and I can't catch up with it.'

His colleague, Dr Florian Mueller, added, 'Here's a new view on robotic technology as a social companion. People haven't really explored that yet, and we think there's huge potential for seeing robots as social companions for exercise.'

Those of you who've seen films such as *Westworld*, *Robocop* or *Blade Runner*, will be acutely aware of the potential dangers malfunctioning (and frequently murderous) robots can pose, but our Australian academics were unperturbed and continued in earnest with the development of 'Joggobot'.

At the time of going to press their baby had yet to make it into mass production, however, and after asking 13 joggers to take the drone out for a 26-minute road test, in truth the feedback on the invention was mixed. The tendency of the 'Joggobot' to occasionally deviate from its aerial path and lead its running companion dangerously off course on the ground was a concern, while other athletic guinea pigs reported they felt, well, a bit silly chasing a flying robot. There were though those who were bowled over by the invention. 'I'm jogging with a robot,' gasped one athlete, 'and people think it's rad.'

The team from Melbourne believe 'Joggobot' could one day also be utilised by lonely cyclists, solitary cross country skiers and rowers with poor social skills They just need to iron out the programming glitches that make their machine occasionally see red and malevolently attempt to lead their runners into the middle of oncoming motorway traffic.

HONESTY OF THE LONG DISTANCE RUNNER

SPAIN, 2013

Sportsmanship is in increasingly short supply these days. As the vertically challenged butcher said to his apprentice after installing an inadvisedly tall fridge, the stakes are just too high, and fair play is today too often sacrificed at the altar of success at all costs.

It is though easy to be too cynical and there remain athletes out there who still value integrity above victory. Obviously we're not talking about Ben Johnson, Justin Gatland, Marion Jones or Asafa Powell, but let's stay upbeat and focus on the good 'uns. Like, for example, Spanish middle distance runner Ivan Fernandez Anaya. He's a good egg. Top drawer really and his story should warm the cockles of even the most curmudgeonly.

Ivan was running in a cross country race near Pamplona in his native Spain. It was a decent field, Ivan was no mean athlete himself and was running in second, but in truth he was getting murdered by the leader, a Kenyan by the name of Abel Mutai, whose CV included the bronze medal in the 3,000m steeplechase at the London Olympics.

The result appeared a foregone conclusion but when Ivan entered the finishing straight and looked into the distance at his rival, he saw that the Kenyan had stopped 10m (33ft) short of the finishing line. Mutai thought he had won but had unwittingly pulled up short.

It wasn't long before Ivan caught up with the stationary

leader, but rather than speed past him and triumphantly break the tape, he stopped. The language barrier between the pair proved a bit of a bugger but after some adroit gesticulation, the Spaniard managed to convey to the Kenyan the nature of his error and Mutai duly finished the race in first place with honest Ivan in second.

'I didn't deserve to win it,' he said. 'I did what I had to do. He was the rightful winner. He created a gap that I couldn't have closed if he hadn't made a mistake. As soon as I saw he was stopping, I knew I wasn't going to pass him. In the race there was hardly anything at stake apart from being able to say that you had beaten an Olympic medallist. But even if they had told me that winning would have earned me a place in the Spanish team for the European Championships, I wouldn't have done it either.

'I also think that I have earned more of a name having done what I did than if I had won. And that is very important, because today, with the way things are in all circles, in soccer, in society, in politics, where it seems anything goes, a gesture of honesty goes down well.'

His noble gesture was almost universally applauded but there were one or two notable dissenters, particularly Ivan's own coach, Martin Fiz. 'It was a very good gesture of honesty,' he said. 'A gesture of the kind that isn't made any more. Or rather, of the kind that has never been made. A gesture that I myself wouldn't have made. I certainly would have taken advantage of it to win. The gesture has made him a better person but not a better athlete. He has wasted an occasion. Winning always makes you more of an athlete. You have to go out to win.'

Lovely guy, Martin, full of the milk of human kindness.

FAILURE TO GO THE DISTANCE

WEST MIDLANDS, 2013

Parks are great places to go for a run. Even in the densest of urban environments, there's invariably an open green space nearby where joggers can escape and enjoy some time away from the traffic and tarmac. The myriad of mothers with prams and the army of angry, small, yappy-type dogs are a drawback, but the fresh air and vistas make it worthwhile overall.

Some parks are of course bigger than others. The largest urban green space in dear old Blighty is Sutton Park in the West Midlands, which boasts an impressive 2,400 acres (971ha), and incidentally it's in the same neck of the woods where you can find the UK's smallest public garden, Prince's Park in the town of Burntwood.

It's absolutely tiny. Minute. Teeny weeny. In fact, it's little more than a triangular traffic island that measures a mere 55 yards (50.3m) all the way around its perimeter, but there's still enough room for a bench and three trees – named Faith, Hope and Charity – and adhering to the old adage of size doesn't matter, the good folk of Burntwood are jolly fond of their bonsai park.

And now we get back to running because in 2013 Prince's Park was the setting for what organisers claimed was the world's shortest ever fun run. An energy-sapping, agonising 55 yards *all the way around* Prince's Park. Suffice to say the paramedics were kept busy that day.

The unusual, one-off event attracted a field of 390 runners, with an age range of between three months and 93 years, and every one proved their stamina by successfully crossing the finishing line. The 'winner' romped home in a rather rapid seven seconds.

'This idea came out of a notion that where could we stage a fun run that everyone, irrespective of age, ability or standard, could take part in,' explained organiser Kevin Wilson. 'The idea to run it around the UK's smallest park was born. We had a good turnout and they all got going around the park, which is just 55 steps in total. Everyone got dressed up and treated it like a normal race.'

The Burntwood fun run has an amusing footnote, causing as it did something of a Transatlantic diplomatic spat. 'The British and the Americans are quarreling – albeit with tongues in cheek – over territory again, this time over who has the world's smallest park, reported the *Associated Press*. 'One, in Portland, Oregon, is essentially a concrete planter, 2ft [61cm] in diameter, with soil and some vegetation, and the *Guinness World Records* says it's the smallest. The other is about 5,000 miles [8,047km] away, in England. Those guys don't claim to have a physically smaller park. But they are disputing whether Portland's is a park at all.'

It was our man Kevin who kicked off the row when he dismissed Mill Ends Park, for that is what the one in Portland is called, as nothing more than 'a glorified flowerpot', in a bid to drum up a bit of publicity for the fun run, and it all snowballed from there with tit for tat jibes from both camps. 'We Americans have a pretty good track record when it comes to taking on the Brits,' said a smart-arsed spokesman for Portland Parks & Recreation. 'Perhaps they're still smarting over that whole American Revolution thing.'

The Yanks sadly had the last laugh. Firstly, *Guinness World Records* stood by their decision that Mill Ends Park was the record holder, and when a local historian pointed out that the park had been officially designated in 1948 'at the behest of city journalist Dick Fagan for snail races' (and that's absolutely true), Portland could also claim to have the world's shortest park-based run. Or at least slide. Kev mumbled something about snails taking a hell of a lot longer than seven seconds to get around but he knew the game was up.

A REFRIGERATED ADVENTURE

UK, 2013

It's a common refrain from runners and non-runners alike that, in the immediate aftermath of the Christmas festivities for example, they find themselves carrying a bit of extra weight. Those pigs in blankets are so moreish, aren't they?

Piling on the pounds is a nightmare for long distance runners in particular, who can ill afford to carry the extra load mile after mile after mile, and it's why you rarely witness 'bigger boned' athletes romping to victory in the marathon.

Endurance runner Tony Phoenix-Morrison takes a different view on the whole weight to performance ratio argument. For our Tony, the heavier the better and this is why he has embarked on a series of exceedingly long runs with a fridge strapped to his back. A fridge that weighs in just shy of 7st (44.5kg).

Tony first hit the headlines when he ran 30 half marathons on 30 consecutive days with the huge Zanussi on his back (he'd wanted Russell Hobbs but Argos had sold out), but that wasn't enough, and he then hit upon the idea of running from John O'Groats to Land's End complete with a Hotpoint behind him (he had traded up by now, John Lewis had a deal on).

Remarkably he made it, running the equivalent of a marathon a day for 40 days in a row to complete the 1,053 mile (1,695km) course, from the northernmost point of mainland Scotland to the southern tip of England. Many long distance runners complain of blisters, but it was Tony's shoulders that were in tatters by the time he finally arrived in Cornwall.

'I took the toughest route that you can do, through London,' he panted at the end of his journey. 'The worst bit was that on day four I fell late at night, I stepped off the road in the darkness. I knocked myself out and broke my left femur. I ran 800 miles [1,287km] with a fractured femur. Hobbled. The whole thing was traumatic from that moment on, it was pure agony.

'When I set out I genuinely had no idea how far I'd get. I wanted to try something so hard that nobody could be certain of its outcome. All I could do was try to prepare myself physically and mentally as best I could. At the end of this I feel humbled really. I've had so much support and generosity from the British public from the top of Scotland all the way down to the bottom of England.'

A couple of footnotes now. If the legal department of Smeg are reading this, we are happy to clarify that Tony did indeed complete his epic run with one of their fine products strapped to his back, and not one of other brands erroneously credited earlier.

Also, do you want to guess what Tony's nickname is? 'Tony the Fridge'? Spot on. When he set out on the whole lugging kitchen appliance around vibe he did toy with the idea of carrying a cooker, but his eight-year-old son quite rightly pointed out that 'Tony the Oven' sounded rubbish and 'Tony the Fridge' was born.

OH DEER!

VIRGINIA, USA, 2013

The Animal Kingdom seemingly abhors runners. We have already related the strange stories of the malevolent moose, crazy kangaroo and badass buzzard, all of whom have launched unprovoked attacks on members of the running community, and such is the volume of beastly incidents out there, it's a wonder athletes ever dare venture beyond their front door.

Our next animal anecdote however is a little different. It still involves the inevitable indignity and injury for the hapless runner in question and the culprit is still a wild beast but this time the creature is entirely blameless. And, as it transpires, stone dead.

Loudon County in the state of Virginia, USA, is the setting for our tale and our fall girl is Krystine Rivera, a 27-year-old administrative analyst who'd had a bad day at work and decided a 7 mile (11.3km) run was in order to sort her head out. How many good days administrative analysts enjoy at work is not relevant right now.

But back to Krystine, who had clocked up five stress-busting miles (8km) when she suddenly heard the screech of a car braking abruptly on the adjacent road. The next few seconds were a blur and she awoke by the side of the road, covered in blood, receiving treatment from paramedics.

So what exactly happened? Was she hit by a speeding Dodge Chrysler with a drunken raccoon at the wheel?

Or was she mowed down by a Cadillac driven by a fugitive beaver?

In fact, poor Krystine had been the victim of an improbable, bizarre accident, which saw a deer make an impromptu and ill-advised attempt to cross the road. The deer didn't make it and was hit by a pensioner driving an SUV, sending the beast flying into the air and, you've guessed it, straight into Krystine.

Unfortunately for her, it was no dainty, Bambi-sized deer that was flung in her direction but a fully fledged buck, and Krystine suffered a concussion, a cut to her scalp and a bruise to her right knee.

'I was running, then I was on the ground and then I was listening to the paramedic,' she said. 'I'm surprised I made it out alive.'

A little melodramatic perhaps, Krystine, but she was certainly more fortunate than her unwitting assailant, a lack of health insurance ensuring the damaged deer received no vital roadside treatment after the accident. 'There were some big vultures flying around,' revealed a local resident the following day, 'and I noticed a dead deer.'

It's tough being a deer in Loudon County. In 2010 alone, more than 5,700 of them were killed during the bloodbath that is the hunting season, but a swift bullet to the head is still a more dignified way to join the animal choir invisible than flying inelegantly through the air towards an unsuspecting administrative analyst.

NAUGHTINESS IN NEW MEXICO

NEW MEXICO, USA, 2013

Answering the sudden and invariably unwelcome call of nature while out for a jog is a dilemma repeatedly faced by many runners. When it's time to go, it's time to go and anyone who finds themselves out on the road when a penny needs to be spent or (sorry about this, we shall be as delicate as possible) another bodily function fulfilled, they can but pray that they are in close proximity to a public convenience or a dense patch of modesty-preserving bushes.

Or, and it's probably prudent to stop reading right now if you're enjoying your tea, you could simply relieve yourself in someone's garden. Repeatedly and in full sight of the bewildered homeowner's CCTV system.

The setting for our unpleasant tale of public defecation – sorry, there really is no more polite way of putting it – is New Mexico, and concerns an understandably irate gentleman who found his backyard the target for an early morning female jogger, who seemingly mistook his property for some kind of *al fresco* WC. Or just didn't give a damn.

Our shameless, phantom pooper was caught on camera doing her beastly business on four separate occasions, breaking off from her run, before hastily pulling up her shorts and speeding off. The fourth time, however, was the final straw and although reluctant to take the matter to the police for fear of not being taken seriously, our disgusted homeowner had had enough of what he described as 'malicious faecal distribution', and released a tape of the jogger to the local TV station in the hope of shaming her into finding a proper toilet.

'She always strikes on weekend mornings,' he told the media. 'She drops her pants, lets go, puts her shorts back up without any wipe, nothing else. This is malicious faecal distribution. She's come back multiple times. This is calculated "look, look, look: I'm dropping my pants as I'm running". If it happens again I'm going to run out there with a hose and hose her down and say "bad human".'

The unedifying clip was duly shown on the gogglebox in the town of Nob Hill where the crime took place (and, no, we're really not making that up), and although no one came forward to unmask the inconsiderate, incontinent jogger, her unwelcome early morning visits to the garden thankfully came to an abrupt halt after the broadcast. Local shopkeepers also reported a dramatic dip in the sales of All Bran in the weeks that followed.

ANGLO-AMERICAN KNITTING WARS

LONDON AND KANSAS, USA, 2013

Knitting and marathon running do not have a vast amount in common. The former is a sedentary activity, traditionally favoured by ladies of a certain age who stopped watching *Countdown* when dear old Richard Whiteley met his maker, while the latter is very much the preserve of high-class athletes and men mired in the midst of a midlife crisis.

There are though countless examples of successful if seemingly unlikely combinations: peanut butter and jelly; Ant and Dec; a sense of social justice and a Conservative Government. Hang on, forget that last one.

Knitting and long distance running joined the club of improbable pairings in the 2000s when a plucky Brit by the name of Susie Hewer was at the forefront of the new craze. Susie got the record-breaking ball rolling in 2008, when she earned her place in the annals of Guinness World Records after knocking out the longest scarf ever produced while running the London Marathon, and she also hit the headlines two years later at the same race when she stitched the longest ever crotchet chain.

Super Susie set a new milestone at the 2013 London Marathon with a 6ft 9in (2.06m) scarf, but by now news of her exploits had crossed the Atlantic, and one of our American cousins decided it was high time Uncle Sam got in on the unusual act.

Susie's Stateside rival was called David Babcock and it is

with regret that we must report that the associate professor of graphic design at the University of Central Missouri absolutely smashed her record in what was only his second ever marathon.

The Kansas City Marathon in 2013 was his first 26-mile race brandishing two knitting needles and a ball of wool, but dextrous David was like a man possessed, and by the time he had crossed the finishing line he was holding a scarf that measured an impressive 12ft 1¾ (3.7m) long. For the record, he completed the course in five hours and 48 minutes, and opted for a fetching combination of orange and purple thread for his record-breaking neck warmer.

'I had discovered Susie Hewer and her world record and thought that it was really cool,' he told the *Runner's World* website. 'My brother-in-law decided that he was going to run the Kansas City Marathon and he wanted company. I waited until he registered and then registered myself. I was thinking besides being supportive of him, how am I going to justify running a slower race. I realised I could do the knitting marathon. So once I had registered, I made my application to *Guinness World Records*. Once I heard back, I had the specific requirements spelled out that I could train to – 30 stitches across in garter stitch, size US 15 needles.

'When the scarf is long enough it wraps around the back of my body and to the front again. It hangs low, around my thighs. It kind of feels like your pants are falling down with the weight low on the legs. With the pace group that helped me keep my time, we would often run a mile, walk a minute. At first I didn't knit during the walks, trying to keep it pure … The record specifies only that you finish in under six hours and as many runners know, "running a marathon" often means walking through aid stations or stopping and staring in a stupor before forcing yourself to move. I think that, if I pressed myself, I could actually get more knitting in there. I could potentially break my own record in both time and in length.'

With the gauntlet firmly thrown down, Susie is already back in training and hoping to reclaim the crown for Britain. She may have lost the battle but the bizarre war of needles, yarn and the hard yards is still to be won.

SWIMWEAR
IN THE ARCTIC
RUSSIA, 2013

Siberia is jolly cold. In the summer months it can reach a reasonably balmy 62.6°F (17°C) but on the whole the Russian region is on the distinctly chilly side and in 2013 a record low temperature of -96°F (-71°C) was recorded in the Siberian village of Oymyakon. Brass monkeys really don't stand a chance in Siberia.

With that climatic information in mind, you might have thought that Russian runners would be some of the most thermally conscious on the planet. Cossack hat? Check. Three layers of Under Armour Cold Gear? Absolutely. Self-heating trainers and gloves worn by cosmonauts on space walks? Why the hell not? It seems though that joggers in the land of Putin, vodka and dancing bears are made of sterner stuff than us fair-weather Westerners and this tale is enough to make you shiver on the spot.

It was March 2013, when average temperatures in the Siberian city of Tomsk can dip as low as 5°F (-15°C), and the snow-covered motorway out of town was heaving with the rush-hour traffic carrying office workers home after another hard day at the Politburo. Progress was slow in the icy conditions but the commute was suddenly and unexpectedly livened up when motorists noticed a shapely young lady jogging in between the cars. A shapely young lady wearing nothing but a pink bikini, a pair of trainers and a big smile.

Where she had come from – or indeed where she was going to – was a mystery, but our Siberian commuters signalled their collective approval of our scantily-clad runner with a chorus of beeping horns and, of course, her appearance was inevitably captured on a series of phone cameras. According to the footage, at one stage she throws in an impromptu, Morecambe and Wise-esque skip and her, frankly insane, run concludes with her celebrating with arms triumphantly outstretched in the air.

The fun and games apparently lasted for less than a minute as she bounced along among startled traffic, but at the risk of stereotyping the Russian authorities, there would have to be repercussions and she was sentenced to six months in a Siberian labour camp. That's not true, she was merely fined by the local traffic police but a labour camp sounds so much more dramatic, doesn't it?

What motivated our athletic bikini-wearer to suddenly take to the motorway in sub-zero conditions is unknown. Again we would not wish to stereotype our Russian friends but we did already mention they're rather partial to the vodka? Just saying.

SATELLITE SAUCINESS
CALIFORNIA, USA, 2014

Technology has revolutionised running in a plethora of ways. It all started in 1979 when Sony released the Walkman, and suddenly joggers everywhere could escape the jaws of angry dogs to the dulcet tones of Michael Jackson or The Police, while today's runners can monitor their own heart rate or keep track of the strides they take, all thanks to the endless wonders of the microchip.

Some of the latest innovations are the GPS tracking apps that allow runners to digitally map out the routes they've taken. Think Etch A Sketch on your laptop recreating the path you've just taken on your jog and you're there.

Now as anyone of a certain age knows, it's impossible to own an Etch A Sketch without secretly drawing something a bit risqué on it. The temptation to spell out a swear word on the screen or create a rude outline is irresistible and, just as generations before used Etch-A-Sketch for surreptitious naughtiness, so modern runners have taken their GPS apps and created filth.

One of the pioneers of this cheeky appropriation of technology is Claire Wyckoff from San Francisco. 'A clever jogger who was tired of her normally monotonous running routes decided to spice things up by turning her runs into doodles,' reported *The Huffington Post* in 2014. 'Claire Wyckoff, a copywriter and comedian, creates her "running drawings" using Nike+, a GPS app which measures distance and maps a jogger's route with a line. Wyckoff's first foray into the medium of run-draw was a depiction of a corgi, which she posted to her Instagram in June.'

Lovely. Claire also 'created' drawings of a classic 8-bit alien from the 1978 Atari game *Space Invaders* and Slimer from the film *Ghostbusters* using her GPS, but what really grabbed the public's attention was her alarmingly detailed depictions of, it's not easy to put this tactfully, gentlemen's love sausages.

That's right, Claire would meticulously plan her runs so that when she came back and plotted where she'd been, the lines of the GPS would create the outline of the family jewels if you will. It may be true that everyone's got to have a hobby but surely there are limits.

Claire's digital phalli were unsurprisingly a big hit with the Internet community and she was even drawn into a Twitter exchange with a potential acolyte who was desperate to know how she achieved such remarkable images. 'It's not easy,' tweeted Claire back. 'First you have to spend a lot of time looking for d***s on maps ... countless hours of d**k searching.'

Funnily enough, many members of the Internet community needed absolutely no encouragement whatsoever to spend countless hours searching for d**ks. Or indeed any kind of genitalia.

SUBTERRANEAN
IN THE CITY
LONDON, 2014

The traffic in London can be murder. Eight million people, all trying to get from A to B angrily clutching their A–Zs, makes congestion a fact of life in the capital, and with the road layout of the city seemingly designed by urban planning's answer to Salvador Dalí, it's a minor miracle anyone ever actually gets anywhere in the Big Smoke. The European Union is currently considering banning the North Circular on the basis that driving on it contravenes the Human Rights Act.

These days an increasing number of Londoners are therefore opting to run hither and thither to avoid the gruesome gridlock. It does mean you tend to get to work a bit sweaty but it's still better than turning up at the office five minutes before home time because you've spent all day stuck on the number 82 bus on the Finchley Road.

This tale however is not one of urbanites jogging to avoid the queues but rather a Londoner actually causing the congestion as a result of an inexplicable run in the wee hours that brought to the capital's traffic to an abrupt and bizarre halt.

It was just past 3 o'clock in the morning on a summer's night when Transport for London employees glanced at the CCTV footage from inside the Blackwall Tunnel and were surprised, to say the least, to see a man jogging along the northbound carriageway clutching a plastic bag. After all, the nineteenth-century route under the River Thames is London's busiest river crossing, with 60,000 cars hurtling through it daily and is strictly off limits to pedestrians and runners alike, and our man's sudden appearance forced TfL to shut the tunnel *tout de suite*. 'The northbound Blackwall Tunnel has been closed,' tweeted TfL somewhat sarcastically, 'due to a pedestrian having a slow jog'.

Scotland Yard's finest were immediately despatched to enquire what the hell our runner thought he was playing at, but our mysterious jogger proved too quick for the boys from the Met, and by the time they arrived on the scene he had made good his escape. 'Our "athlete" made it,' tweeted TfL. 'A dreadful time, but hey, at least he has gone.'

Those caught in the tailbacks caused by the closure of the tunnel were not quite as amused as the wags at TfL but some did turn to social media to vent their frustration. 'Let the traffic in,' suggested one stationary commuter, 'I'm sure it'll turn into a sprint'.

Despite London being one of the most CCTV-heavy cities in the world, the identity of the ill-advised jogger was never established or indeed whether he was running to or from something (or somebody) in particular. We don't even know what was in the mysterious plastic bag but it definitely was not an acute sense of direction or self-preservation.

THE COTTONTAIL
CLAPHAM INTERLOPER
LONDON, 2014

In terms of its ability to generate excitement among the younger members of society, Easter bows only to the behemoth that is Christmas and birthdays in the anticipation stakes. Kids love chocolate and therefore adore Easter and the smorgasbord of cocoa-based confectionery it brings with it annually.

The kids of Clapham in south London were certainly licking their lips at the prospect of the big day as it approached in 2014. They just couldn't wait to get their mitts on all those Easter eggs, but the build-up was given a mysterious extra dimension when local parents and their offspring noticed a giant white rabbit jogging around Clapham Common.

'Is that the Easter Bunny?' the kids asked breathlessly as the running rabbit made regular appearances over the fortnight leading up to Easter Sunday, but mum and dad didn't have a clue. In fact, mum and dad became rather alarmed by the enormous bunny, and many took to social media to appeal for more information about the beast of the Common as absolutely no one dubbed it.

'We received messages from some of our Clapham mum members about this person dressed as a rabbit running around,' said the editor of a local lifestyle website. 'This isn't all that normal, even around Easter. The kids absolutely loved it but we were a bit baffled as to what they were doing. Some of them have only just learnt about Easter Bunny so were quite thrilled to see it exercising around the park.'

Concerned parents debated whether to call in David Attenborough to help solve the mystery, but he was in Venezuela trying to film the mating rituals of the notoriously elusive lesser-spotted fungus beetle and couldn't be contacted. In the end, however, our bunny unmasked herself and it turned out to be one Elle Linton, a fitness blogger who, in a nice piece of thematic symmetry, just happened to be in training for the upcoming Clapham Rabbit Run.

'I was just doing a bit of training,' she said. 'I will be doing 5K dressed as a rabbit on the day so I had to get used to running in the suit, instead of my usual gear. I want to raise a good deal of money for charity but I am a competitor at heart and so had to get myself used to the demands of the rabbit outfit.'

Elle is of course not the first 'rabbit' to make an appearance in these pages, and if you cast your mind back to the tale entitled 'Run Rabbit, Run (1994)' you will remember the story of the unheralded pace setter Paul Pilkington who upset the odds to win the Los Angeles Marathon in 1994. Rabbits, it seems, are addicted to running even if not being chased by foxes, harassed by famers or pursuing their fifth amorous encounter of the day.

COLOURS OF THE RAINBOW

CHESHIRE, 2014

A single letter can make an awful lot of difference to the meaning of a sentence or phrase. Take, for example, *Run or Die: The Inspirational Memoir of the World's Greatest Ultra-Runner*, which is a book written by Spaniard Kílian Jornet and, as the title suggests, all about his extraordinary feats of arduous athletic endurance. The Run or Dye 5K however, while still concerned with the realms of running, is something altogether different, less gruelling and rather more fun.

Based on the ancient Hindu festival of Holi, and introduced to the UK from the States, Run or Dye runs see competitors bombarded with coloured dye along the length of the course, and by the time they reach the finishing line, they tend to make Joseph's amazing technicolour dreamcoat look rather monotone by comparison.

'This is your chance to have the most colour-filled day of your life with family and friends as you celebrate life, friendship, fitness, and fun,' boasts the Run or Dye website. 'Whether you're a recovering couch potato or an avid marathon runner, you'll love the atmosphere and experience. At Run or Dye, you become part of the rainbow.

'As you run, walk, dance through the course, you will get showered in safe, eco-friendly, plant-based powdered dye at every kilometre, turning you into a technicolour canvas of fun. While the dye is designed to be washable, we don't do your laundry, so we recommend that you wear something you don't mind getting a little colourful. And just when you thought you couldn't possibly be more colourful, you'll cross the finish line and find yourself in the middle of a colour storm at our Dye Festival.'

The British version of the American Rainbow Splash 5K, which was held in over 150 cities in the USA before being exported across the Atlantic, Run or Dye debuted at Cholmondeley Castle in Cheshire in 2014, and is now a firm fixture on the running calendar with races up and down the country.

It's been quite the hit with fun runners but should you be a particularly well-coiffured runner who is concerned about their 'do', it may sadly not be the event for you.

'The dye is made of coloured corn starch and is designed to be washable,' warn the organisers. 'If you have light-coloured hair, or if it's expected to be rainy or a particularly humid day, try adding some leave-in conditioner to your hair before the run. If you are particularly concerned about your hair we advise you to keep it covered throughout or consult your hairdresser for pre-run hair advice.'

THE ELEMENTS STRIKE BACK

OREGON, USA, 2014

Most joggers greet the first fall of winter snow with a familiar sigh of resignation. Of all that Mother Nature can conjure up, the icy white stuff is perhaps the hardest to battle from a runner's perspective, and no matter how tentative the step, adhesive the grip of the trainer or seemingly obstacle-free the route ahead, a slippery mishap is never far away.

This was illustrated with hilarious results by a hapless jogger in Portland, Oregon, USA, who made two catastrophic mistakes when the snow began to descend from on high on the city in 2014. Her first error of judgement was to lace up her trainers in the first place, her second was to stop and have a chat with a local TV news station about the joys of running in the snow. It is of course unedifying to take pleasure in another's misfortune but what happened next was pure comedy gold.

Our unlucky lady was Chelsea, who was out for a jog with her beau, Michael. The pair were asked for an interview by a TV reporter doing the obligatory piece on how the locals were coping with snowmageddon and why our love birds were out running.

'It's the perfect texture for running,' enthused Chelsea. 'Very low impact and it's dry snow so your feet don't get wet.'

'It's been a lot of fun,' chipped in Michael. 'There's a lot of other runners but more skiers than runners for sure.

I think they've got a little bit of advantage with the whole stride and glide thing. It's too nice to not be out here.'

Interview over and out. The reporter then thanked them for taking the time to chat and Chelsea and Michael headed off down the road. The camera followed them eagerly, capturing the blizzard raging around the pair, but just before the cameraman decided to call it a day, Chelsea slipped. Her arms went out instinctively to steady herself but it was already too late and she was over, hitting the tarmac with her derrière as inelegantly as you can imagine. That, as they say, has got to hurt.

The real indignity however was the fact that it had all been captured on film. The residents of Portland all had a good laugh when they tuned in for the news that evening, but of course the clip quickly went viral and poor old Chelsea was a reluctant Internet sensation, another victim of the inclement elements. Clips of her embarrassing misfortune on a popular video website you may have visited previously were variously titled 'Portland Jogger Snow Fail', 'Runners get taste of irony' and, rather cruelly, 'Hilarious! Jogger Tells TV reports "snow is perfect for running" and falls on HER BUTT live.' Ouch.

To her credit though Chelsea was able to see the funny side. 'We ran by this reporter and cameraman who looked like they'd been stuck waiting for something to happen for a while,' she said. 'Given that there were actual cross country skiers in the streets and even a few hardcore cyclists, a pair of runners was probably pretty lame. But maybe we were just the only people who stopped when they called after us.

'All I can say is that running in powder when there's no one else out at night is a load of fun. But stopping to pose for the local news station in the middle of the icy street hurts like a bitch. Glad it's as funny for everyone else as it was for us.

'My neck was a little sore but the ridiculous, awesome irony of the situation cushioned the blow pretty well. The ground was really uneven on the hill where they had us standing and my eyes were still splotchy from the light on the camera. We were actually trying to get back to where it was all powdery and soft when I bit it on that patch of ice.'

So it was actually the reporter's fault for luring Chelsea and Michael off the snow and onto the hazardous ice. Once again, the media has much to answer for.

RUNNERS' ROAD RAGE
INDIA, 2014

Runners and cars are not the best of friends. Joggers curse motorists when they park their gas guzzlers on their precious pavement while drivers cannot abide having to swerve to avoid runners on their treasured tarmac. The mutual suspicion turns to outright loathing when the god of traffic lights favours one group over the other at a junction. No, the gel-cushioned running shoe and the internal combustion engine are not bezzies on Facebook.

The animosity that lingers between the two camps was only exacerbated after the staging of the Bangalore Half Marathon in 2014, an event that degenerated into farce when the elite athletes in the field put their trust in the car but were ultimately to regret their misplaced faith in four wheels.

The race initially got off to a perfect start and just over 9 miles (15km) a breakaway group of runners had moved clear of the chasing pack. The leaders were following the race car, and for another 15 minutes they dug deep and ploughed ahead, but the crowd had disappeared and the alarm bells started ringing. The car had failed to make a planned U-turn back down the course to take the athletes in the direction of the finishing line and they were in the middle of nowhere and out of the race.

'There were no officials on the road where we were supposed to take the U-turn,' Inderjit Patel, one of the front runners, told *The Times of India*. 'We couldn't find any event organizers nearby. We were just following the pilot car and we had covered around 20km [12½ miles] in one hour as we were going at a pace of two minutes, 59 seconds per kilometre [⅔ mile]. It was too late when we were told what had happened. There was no point continuing the race. I am not bothered about missing the prize money but disappointed that we had to suffer this humiliation.'

That however was not the end of their humiliation. The lead car slunk off in shame, leaving our elite runners stranded, and they were forced to rely on the generosity of fellow runners and public transport to get themselves back to race HQ.

'Probably after the 15km [9⅓ mile] mark we had doubts whether the route was correct,' said Soji Mathew, another one of our 'misguided' leaders. 'We had to beg for 20 rupees as we didn't have any money with us. Luckily some morning joggers helped us and also guided us to the nearest metro station. We took a train to reach the station closest to the finishing line.'

The race organisers offered their profuse apologies for the spectacular cock-up, but Patel, Mathew and Co. weren't listening and were last seen heading in the direction of the garage housing the race cars, clutching between them a Stanley knife, sledgehammer and crow bar.

They, however, were not the only victims of poor organisation that day, and one female athlete running the full marathon somehow managed to cover 3 miles (5km) in the wrong direction, before officials pointed out the error of her ways. Please feel free to insert your own jokes about women's sense of direction. We of course would not be so ungallant.

JAPAN'S FUTURISTIC FRUIT

JAPAN, 2015

As every runner knows, bananas are an excellent source of fuel. The lovely yellow fellas are positively bursting at the seams with precious carbohydrates, they're great at boosting blood sugar levels and they even come pre-wrapped for convenience. And if all that wasn't enough, they're without equal if you're a cartoon character, and you need someone to take a tumble.

The only problem with bananas is that they are very twentieth century, very analogue in a digital age. If only there was some way of combining a 'nana's natural goodness with some cutting edge technology, of creating a synergy between fruit and the microchip. Of, perhaps, pimping a banana with the twenty-first century runner in mind.

It was a challenge clever bods in white coats just couldn't resist, and at the Tokyo Marathon of 2015, two of the field wore what was proudly billed as the 'world's first edible wearable', aka a real banana implanted with an LED that could display an athlete's heart rate, tweets from supporters and also featured a built-in GPS.

Amazing eh? The best part however, was the promise that at the end of their gruelling 26 miles 385 yards, the wearer of the banana could simply peel back the skin and feast on the fruit's flesh.

'Dole has created an amazing new banana, the Wearable Banana,' boasted the breathless promotional video for the fruit of the future. 'Engineers have tested it day in, day out to come up with this amazing device. This is no regular banana. It's the best companion for any marathoner. You can strap it around your wrist and run with it until you finish the race. And understanding the wearable fad occurring around the world, this device can also detect your running time, heart rate and advise you when to eat bananas on your run. After you cross the finishing line of course you can eat it too.'

Hang on a minute. How exactly do you strap a banana around your wrist? Who really needs advice on when to eat bananas? And who are these mysterious Dole people?

Further investigation reveals Dole are no more than the Japanese equivalent of Fyffes, a wholesale importer of bananas, and the Wearable Banana was no more than a PR stunt in an on-going war with a ketchup company called Kagome, a purveyor of tomatoes to the Japanese public.

The hostilities began because Dole had the gig as the official sponsors of the Tokyo Marathon. Every year, as part of the deal, they supplied runners with thousands upon thousands of free bananas, but Kagome wanted athletes to turn to tomatoes as their athletic snack of choice.

They hit upon a bit of disturbing guerrilla marketing to get their message across, entering a runner into the marathon with a red robot mounted on his shoulders. More disturbingly still, the robot would intermittently reach behind the runner's back with its metal arms, grab a tomato from its stash and then place it in the athlete's mouth. The Wearable Banana was Dole's PR counter punch.

Fortunately, the marathon was not sponsored by Nippon Suisan Kaisha, which is one of Japan's biggest squid, octopus and assorted seafood companies.

NGETICH ON HER KNEES
CHINA, 2015

The runners of Kenya are rather famous for their athletic prowess. Kenyans are renowned worldwide for their grace, speed and stamina over middle and long distances, and they have amassed more medals over the years than an avaricious magpie let loose in the Imperial War Museum. The Kenyans just can't stop winning.

At the World Athletics Championships in Beijing in 2015, for example, Kenya's finest helped themselves to seven gold, six silver and three bronze medals to finish top of the pops and relegate the mighty Jamaica and the USA into second and third respectively.

Yes, Kenyan athletes are jolly good runners indeed but even they have their bad days at the office, and the Austin Marathon in Texas in 2015 proved to be the shift from hell for elite competitor Hyvon Ngetich, as she desperately attempted to complete the 26 miles, 385 yards.

All was well in the 29-year-old's world going past the 25 mile (40.2km) mark but, with a mere 400m (437 yards) to go to the finish, Hyvon suddenly collapsed onto the tarmac. Medics rushed to her with a wheelchair, but Hyvon knew the rules, her race was over if she accepted any help whatsoever, and she decided to carry on. The problem was she couldn't get back on her feet and so, to the cheers of the crowd, she crawled all the way to the finish line on her hands and knees, her forehead occasionally scraping on the road, such was her level of exhaustion. She did sacrifice second place in the race as a result of her unconventional finish but that really wasn't the point.

'Oh, God, thank you, I crossed,' she told *BBC World Service Radio* after the race. 'For the last 2km [3⅕ miles], I don't remember. Finish line … I have no idea. Running, always, you have to keep going, going. I can't remember what happened and I didn't see the finish line. I don't remember all that crawling or whatever. Even the collapsing I don't remember.'

Medical checks revealed her exhaustion – and obvious amnesia – were the result of dangerously low blood sugar levels, but Hyvon's heroics did earn her more than just the crowd's admiration. For a start, despite her collapse, she still finished the women's race in third, which in turn secured her a coveted place at the Boston Marathon. She was also not left out of pocket after her misfortune.

'You have run the bravest race and crawled the bravest crawl I have ever seen in my life,' said race director John Conley. 'When you came around the corner on your hands and knees, I have never, in 43 years of being involved in this sport, seen a finish like that. You have earned much honour, and I am going to adjust your prize money, so you can get the prize money you would have gotten if you were second.'

Kerching! What was not made clear by our spontaneously generous race official was whether the real runner-up, local girl Hannah Steffan, would have to settle for a reduction in her purse, or whether both athletes would pick up equivalent cheques. Hyvon was too knackered to argue while Hannah was still fuming at surrendering second place because she'd been stupid enough to remain standing.

MAKING MUSIC
ON THE MOVE
AUSTRALIA, 2015

There are many things runners can return home with after their athletic exertions. Blisters or a twisted ankle rank amongst the least welcome end products post-jog, while an endorphin-fuelled sense of well being, or a new personal best for 10K (6¼ miles) are definitely high on the athlete's wish list. A new career in music however is definitely not one of the traditional upshots of lacing up your trainers and knocking out a few brisk miles.

And yet that's just what happened when a chap called Ross Burbury was out jogging in sunny Brisbane in 2015 and suddenly had his run interrupted by a couple of DJs brandishing a keyboard and microphone. The musical duo called themselves Mashd N Kutcher, and asked our Ross whether he fancied knocking out a tune for them, although they neglected to tell him it was for a compilation video of people performing on the streets they planned to release online.

Ross proved himself game when he accepted the invitation, but old Mashd and Kutch's jaws hit the floor when he belted out a brilliant song he'd written himself called 'Passenger', a soulful piano-based ballad. Think Aussie Ed Sheeran and you wouldn't be a million miles away. The subsequent video got more than 1.25 million views within a week of being uploaded and Ross was the undisputed star of the compilation.

'All we wanted to do was show you there is talent everywhere, not just on the TV and radio,' said Matt, one half of Mashd N Kutcher. 'We were pretty shocked. We had been approaching people all afternoon, and suddenly we found someone who not only sings but is willing to bust out like that on the first try.

'As DJs we try to collaborate with as many people as we can, but it's not always easy to link up with Black Eyed Peas or David Guetta, so we decided to hit the streets. We're pretty stoked at how much the video has taken off. It's very exciting. Hopefully we can do something for the singer too, it would be amazing if he got signed.'

The whole experience certainly came as a surprise to Ross, minding his own business as he was while on his jog, but he'd just watched *Dead Poets Society* and he resolved to *carpe diem*. 'I was really shocked,' he said. 'I had no idea what they had planned for that video but I plan to release a solo EP later this year with 'Passenger' as one of the songs. The lesson is take every chance you get presented with. You never know where you'll end up.'

(Almost) true to his word, Ross did record and release 'Passenger' as a single in 2015, complete with accompanying video, and although at the time of going to press it has yet to become a worldwide hit to rival, say, compatriot Jason Donovan's seminal 'Sealed With a Kiss', Ross had at least got a foot in the music industry door thanks initially to his love of jogging.

THE SCIENCE OF ATTRACTION

UK, 2015

If you'd care to cast your mind back a few pages, you may remember that there is a school of scientific thought that maintains that the number of miles you run each week can play a significant role in determining the sex of your child (see 'Let's Talk About Sex, Baby').

It's a fascinating theory but we must address another, albeit similar, study which maintains that how far you run can actually dictate, if you'll pardon the potty mouth, how much sex you get. More specifically, the research suggests that male long distance runners are more attractive to the ladies than fellas who get out of breath after a 200m huff and puff to the corner shop. And it's nothing to do with bulging calf muscles, toned forearms or washboard abs.

The study was carried out by clever bods from the University of Cambridge and University College London, who analysed 542 male competitors taking part in the Robin Hood Half Marathon and discovered in essence that the better the runner, the more likely they were to have the opposite sex swooning at their feet.

'Long-distance running may be a lonely pastime – but academics say that men who can run for miles may find it easier to attract women,' reported the *Daily Mail*. 'People who are better at running half marathons are likely to have been exposed to high levels of testosterone in the womb, researchers from Cambridge University said. This means they not only have better cardiovascular efficiency but also a strong sex drive and high sperm count – suggesting that historically they were chosen by women as more desirable mates.

'This may be because "persistence hunting" – exhausting prey by tirelessly tracking it – was a vital way to get food. It means that men who could run long distance were more attractive to women – a trait the researchers say has persisted through the generations.'

The boffins discovered by photocopying the runners' hand prints and measuring race times and other data that the best half marathoners tended to have longer ring fingers, which is often a sign that they had been exposed to higher than average levels of hormone in the womb.

'The observation that endurance running ability is connected to reproductive potential in men suggests that women in our hunter-gatherer past were able to observe running as a signal for a good breeding partner,' explained Dr Danny Longman, the lead researcher on the study. 'It was thought that a better hunter would have got more meat, and had a healthier – and larger – family as a consequence of providing more meat for his family.'

Don't forget, it was in the days before you could order a couple of burgers or a rack of ribs online from Tesco. You didn't have to sing for your supper but you did have to chase your lunch.

Marathoners the length and breadth of the country universally welcomed the conclusions of the ground-breaking study, claiming that it proved what they'd known all along – runners are total sexpots with the prettiest wives and girlfriends.

THE FIREMAN'S DASH
SOUTH WALES, 2015

'By failing to prepare,' Benjamin Franklin once warned, 'you are preparing to fail.' The Founding Father and one-time Vice President of the USA definitely had a point, and who here among us, for example, hasn't come to regret not taking proper precautions for the zombie apocalypse (bottled water, clean socks, pump action shotgun etc.), only to see hordes of the undead marching menacingly towards the front door.

Despite Benjamin's advice, however, there are those who persist in a very 'relaxed' approach to preparation, and one such chancer in the athletic sphere is Kevin Summerhayes, a fireman from Wales, who decided on something of a whim to enter the Cardiff Half Marathon in 2015. To make things interesting our Kev thought he'd attempt the 13-plus miles (21.1km) wearing his full firefighter's uniform – helmet, steel-capped, knee-high boots, tunic and leggings, the works – around 2st (12.7kg) worth of extra weight.

By his own admission his training regime was not exactly rigorous. In fact, Kevin only went out for three light jogs before the half marathon because 'the sweat and discomfort did not make me want to practise', and he turned up at the start line in his uniform more in hope than anticipation.

Now, if you are expecting Kev's lack of preparation to come back and bite him in the derrière at this point you are going to be sorely disappointed, because he did in fact fly around the course despite his heavy footwear and energy-sapping gear. Obviously he had to endure every second spectator hilariously shouting out 'Where's the fire?' as he ran past, but that was to be expected.

His time in Cardiff was one hour and 52 minutes and 45 seconds. To put this into context, an Austrian by the name of Herbert Kreen had covered the same distance in the same firefighter's uniform at the Oberbank Half Marathon in Linz just six months earlier, and *Guinness World Records* had recognised his time of one hour and 55 minutes and 57 seconds as a world record.

And this is where Kev's lack of preparation did come back to haunt him. Despite running more than three minutes quicker than his Austrian rival, Kev had failed to notify *Guinness World Records* of his possible attempt on the record 12 weeks before the race and, rules being rules, they refused to ditch Kreen and anoint him as the new, official fastest fireman in the West.

Kevin was fuming with himself but insisted there was a 'strong possibility' of him making another attempt on the record in the future, having of course first notified the jobsworths at *Guinness World Records* in triplicate.

TERROR IN TAIWAN

TAIWAN, 2015

Marathons with a reputation for producing fast times are enduringly popular with runners. The chance of registering a new personal best appeals to the ego of any self-respecting athlete and many organisers will go to great lengths to ensure their particular race presents entrants with the opportunity to run quicker than they have ever done before.

Obviously it's frowned upon to simply cut the length of the course from its iconic 26 miles 385 yards, but there are plenty of other (legitimate) ploys to speed things up a bit. Ensuring there are no energy-sapping climbs *en route* is of course a no-brainer, while staging the race when the climatic conditions are most favourable and runners are not roasted under the midday sun another. The jury remains out on the benefits of lashings of free Red Bull or Lucozade.

The organisers of the Keelung Marathon in Taiwan, however, opted for a rather more surreal approach to getting athletes to run faster in 2015 and decided fear was what was required to bring out the X factor in competitors. Fear and a young actress dressed up as a ghost.

The plan was as simple as it was bizarre. Costumed in a red dress, clutching an umbrella and her face covered in suitably ghoulish white make-up and eyes blackened with heavy mascara, the spectre waited for unsuspecting runners at the halfway point of the marathon and chased for a few yards all those she felt were slacking off. It was, insisted the organisers, a genius way of delivering a deluge of personal bests, while our ghostly motivator insisted she didn't want to give anyone a heart attack. 'I didn't dare frighten people by hiding in the woods,' she told reporters. 'I just waited for them to encourage them.'

The results in truth were mixed. Some unwitting runners were indeed terrified by the appearance of the ghoul and, fuelled by a sudden surge in adrenalin, noticeably quickened their pace, but there were others who lost significant time as a result of falling to the ground in fits of hysterical laughter. Mercifully, there were no heart attacks.

It was not the actress's first appearance on the day of the Keelung Marathon. Prior to her attempt at macabre motivation, and for reasons organisers evidently kept to themselves, she took to the stage for the opening ceremony dressed as a green and yellow dinosaur (wearing pink trainers). It was nowhere near as scary a turn as her subsequent portrayal of a ghost in the red dress but at least it didn't reduce the younger racers to floods of tears.

THE STYROFOAM SOS

MICHIGAN, USA, 2015

Running at night can be a perilous pastime. It doesn't matter how many lumens your head torch boasts, how well illuminated the streets you jog along are or indeed how many carrots you've eaten, it's dark at night and danger can lurk everywhere. The problem is that you've got bugger all chance of seeing it coming.

And so it was for a hapless jogger from Michigan who popped on her trainers and headed out one bracing October evening for her run. All was well in her world until, in the fading light, she unwittingly stepped on and dislodged a drain cover by the side of a road and tumbled 8ft (2.4m) down the hole she'd accidentally exposed. She was stuck waist deep in freezing water and, having neglected to bring her mobile with her, she had no way of calling for help. To make matters even worse, the enveloping darkness meant passing motorists were oblivious to the 33-year-old's predicament and no one stopped to investigate.

Things were looking bleak for our partially submerged jogger. She was too deep in the hole for her arm to stretch up to road level, but she was nothing if not inventive and, noticing a discarded piece of Styrofoam packaging floating in the drain water, she grabbed the flotsam and began waving it frantically to attract attention. She was in the water for two hours but finally a passing car spied her signal and stopped.

The good Samaritans – Jay Niewiek and Brandon Noorman – were initially bemused by the sight of a piece of rubbish poking up from the storm drain, but when they got out of their motor to take a closer look, they came across our sodden damsel in distress. She was relieved to see them to say the least and told Jay and Brandon that 20 cars had passed her by before they finally came to her rescue.

'It was crazy, it looked a little strange,' Brandon told reporters after answering the surreal SOS. 'But then we noticed a hand connected to a piece of Styrofoam. She was just like "Thank you, I'm so cold". I was shivering just watching her. It was certainly cold.'

The police and paramedics were summoned and although she had suffered cuts and bruises to the head in her unscheduled plunge down the hole, the jogger didn't need hospital treatment and headed home for a hot bath and a cup of Horlicks. Jay and Brandon spent the rest of the week regaling the media with tales of their heroism while our lady runner eschewed the spotlight but doubtless vowed to never again hit the road after three in the afternoon.

LEROY'S UNLIKELY MARATHON

PENNSYLVANIA, USA, 2015

Most marathons offer at least one human-interest story the media can greedily seize upon. With races boasting fields in the thousands, there's invariably someone with a tale to tell and we are all *au fait* with stories of entrants running to raise funds for the local cat sanctuary, to shame erstwhile classmates who called them fatty boom-boom, or to prove it is possible to run the 26 miles 385 yards while wearing a bright pink spandex jump suit and high heels. And that's just the men.

The Harrisburg Marathon in Pennsylvania in 2015 was like shooting fish in a barrel for the local press. There were of course ample runners in ridiculous costumes to keep the photographers occupied but it was a definite case of hold the front page when a husband and wife duo romped home in first place in the men's and women's events respectively.

Fred Joslyn came home in two hours, 30 minutes and 43 seconds to claim the men's title, and when his missus Shelby crossed the finishing line around 40 minutes later as the fastest woman on the course, the media boys knew they had a story on their hands. The married marathoners happily fielded a barrage of questions about their domestic bliss, athletic exploits and whether they ever got their running shorts mixed up in the dirty washing, and the hacks rapidly retired to the nearest watering hole.

The real story, however, was the exploits of a young chap

called Leroy Stolzfus who recorded a time of three hours, five minutes and 45 seconds. Nothing remarkable there, but what was highly unusual was the fact Leroy had run the entire race wearing old-fashioned trousers, braces and a long-sleeved, button-down blue shirt.

If his outfit sounds familiar it's because Leroy is Amish and he decided to attempt the race in traditional attire. He did nod to modernity by donning a pair of trainers but otherwise he kept things distinctly old school as he embarked on the marathon. It was an impressive performance for a runner dressed like your granddad and he was actually less than a minute shy of a time that would have qualified him for the Boston Marathon.

'I was feeling good but I kind of almost crashed at mile 15,' the Amish youngster said. 'I had no pain whatsoever. It was more mental anguish than in my legs. You have to train yourself not to think about it. It will just slow you down. I was once told by someone that it's 20 per cent training and 80 per cent mental. I do believe that now.'

By day Leroy explained he was a tobacco shop worker who clocked on at six every morning. To get to work he walked a mile [1.6km] to and from the bus stop, the nearest transport link to his Amish community, and he admitted that his arduous schedule meant his preparations for the race were not exactly thorough.

'Sometimes I don't even get 10 miles [16.1km] training in before a marathon,' he said. 'It's a natural talent but I do a lot more training than I used to. How can I do this if I don't train that much? I think the type of work I do, lifting all day, and all the walking really helps.'

BIBLIOGRAPHY

BOOKS

The Olympics: A Very Peculiar History, David Arscott,
Book House, 2015

*Deerfoot, Athletics' Noble Savage: From Indian
Reservation to Champion of the World*, Rob Hadgraft,
Desert Island, 2012

*The Little Wonder: The Untold Story of Alfred Shrubb
World Champion Runner*, Rob Hadgraft, Desert Island
Books Limited, 2004

*Lancashire Legends, Traditions, Pageants, Sports With
an Appendix Containing a Rare Tract on the Lancashire
Witches*, John Harland and Thomas Turner Wilkinson,
Ulan Press, 2012

Sports Around the World: History, Culture, and Practice,
John Nauright, ABC-CLIO, 2012

*Operation Goodtime and the Battle of the Treasury Islands,
1943*, Reg Newell, McFarland, 2012

*Can We Have Our Balls Back, Please? How the British
Invented Sport,* Julian Norridge, Penguin, 2008

Great Olympic Moments, Sir Steve Redgrave, Headline,
2011

*Anything for a T-Shirt: Fred Lebow and the New York City
Marathon, the World's Greatest Footrace*, Ron Rubin,
Syracuse University Press, 2004

Running Through The Ages, Edward S. Sears, McFarland & Co. Inc., 2009

Marathon 490BC: The First Persian Invasion of Greece, Nick Sekunda, Greenwood Press, 2005

A Handy Book of Curious Information, William Shepard Walsh, Nabu Press, 2010

The Marathon Monks of Mount Hiei, John Stevens, Echo Point Books & Media, 2013

Marathon Woman: Running the Race to Revolutionize Women's Sports, Kathrine Switzer, Da Capo Press Inc, 2009

Running On Empty, Marshall Ulrich, Avery, 2012

Funny Running Shorts, Geoff Wightman and Dave Bedford, Descartes Publishing Ltd, 2003

WEBSITES

www.bbc.co.uk
www.dailymail.co.uk
www.history.com
www.historynewsnetwork.org
www.mensrunninguk.co.uk
www.royalalberthall.com
www.runnersworld.com
www.runningpast.com
www.strangehistory.net
www.telegraph.co.uk
www.wsj.com

OTHER TITLES IN

THE STRANGEST® SERIES

The *Strangest* series has been delighting and enthralling readers for decades with weird, exotic, spooky and baffling tales of the absurd, ridiculous and the bizarre. This range of fascinating books – from Football to London, Rugby to Law and many subjects in between – details the very curious history of each one's funniest, oddest and most compelling characters, locations and events.

9781910232910   9781910232866

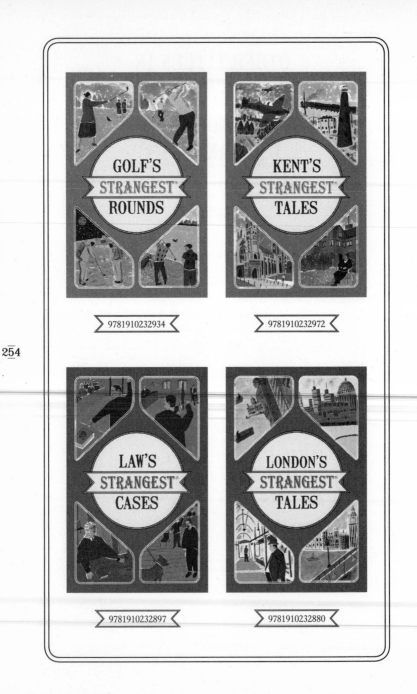

GOLF'S STRANGEST ROUNDS
9781910232934

KENT'S STRANGEST TALES
9781910232972

LAW'S STRANGEST CASES
9781910232897

LONDON'S STRANGEST TALES
9781910232880

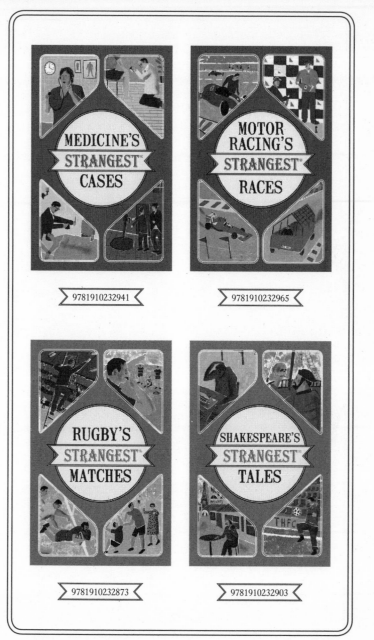

MEDICINE'S STRANGEST CASES
9781910232941

MOTOR RACING'S STRANGEST RACES
9781910232965

RUGBY'S STRANGEST MATCHES
9781910232873

SHAKESPEARE'S STRANGEST TALES
9781910232903

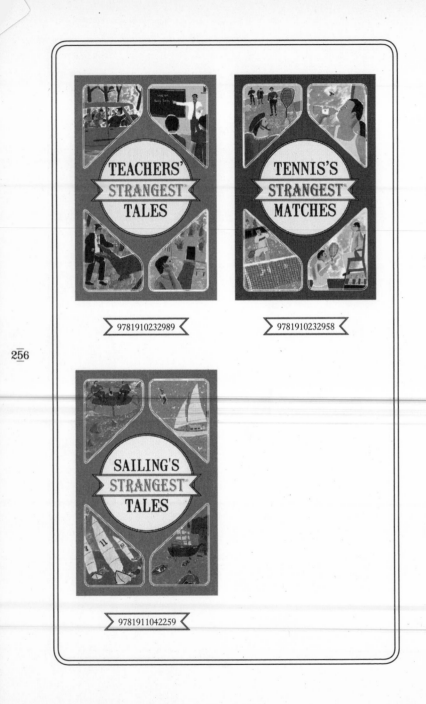